AT HOME
WITH UMAMI

For anyone in pursuit of deliciousness

AT HOME WITH UMAMI

HOME-COOKED RECIPES UNLOCKING THE MAGIC OF SUPER-SAVOURY DELICIOUSNESS

Laura Santtini

PHOTOGRAPHY BY CON POULOS

RYLAND PETERS & SMALL
LONDON • NEW YORK

INTRODUCTION

Ever since I can remember I have been fascinated by flavours and the feelings they evoke. I can recall literally 'tasting' my life long before I could even voice those tastes. Over the years, flavours and feelings have become rather more than just a fascination for me, and I am now lucky enough to pursue a career in which the two meet, sometimes in conflict but never apart.

So why umami? That is the question I am often asked – and, aside from the obvious 'why not?', the truth is that umami is the ultimate expression of flavour, although hitherto the least understood of the five basic tastes. It is for this reason that umami seemed like the perfect cornerstone upon which a lifelong flavourist such as myself might begin gingerly to build a temple to taste and flavour.

A gourmet oxymoron, umami is both ubiquitous and elusive, present but often unrecognized. I call it 'the sexy flavour', because it is the taste that keeps on giving long after its fellow basic tastes – sweet, salty, sour and bitter – are spent. Umami is that extra mouthful-ness that makes us go 'mmmmm'; to taste umami is to savour the savoury long after the morsel itself has disappeared. It is savoury deliciousness on a plate and on the palate.

Once understood, umami is your best friend both in and out of the kitchen. It's a total game-changer for cooks of all levels who want to grab life with both hands and lick it! This book explores the power of umami at home, as it is experienced domestically in daily lives all over the world. I have deliberately kept the complex science and chemistry behind umami to a minimum and have included only what is needed to enjoy and understand umami in a domestic context. I have, however, included a source for a wealth of scientific information on page 8. The mission of this book is to assist the reader to make food that is unexpectedly more delicious through the magic of umami. I hope that once you have bitten, you will be forever smitten…

FLAVOURS & FEELINGS

I can clearly remember the day that flavours and feelings became inextricably linked in my mind and the extraordinary thought process that triggered my life's work.

I was sitting cross-legged on my bedroom floor in front of a full-length mirror trying to make myself cry. I had just seen a movie where the star had cried at every feeling she felt from delight to despair, and I wanted to know what it felt like to be able to let it all out like that. From grazed knees to a bruised ego, no tears had ever dared to betray my feelings – I was too proud for the world to know how easily it could hurt me. This was different, though – it was a controlled experiment and I was alone in the lab.

I remember slowly fading out the last harrowing *Lassie* scene whilst sticking out an enquiring tongue. Those sad black and white scenes had coaxed a couple of puffy tears to spill from my eyes and snowball towards my mouth in slow motion, and as I drew the tear back into my mouth, I knew that the experiment had worked; for the first time in my life I had knowingly tasted a feeling and logged it for what it really was. I concluded that God had made tears clear and unreadable, so that the salty emotions they carried would be invisible to the naked eye. I understood that only my tongue and my tummy could tell my brain of the feelings suspended in these salty spheres. I pondered that tears of joy would taste different to tears of despair because they had to be made with a spoonful of sugar, and that the forced tears currently talking to my tongue had been borrowed from crocodiles for the purpose of the experiment. That afternoon, salt and sadness had formed a bond on my cheek that was to become the purpose of my life.

The taste of tears was quickly replaced with the taste of great excitement as I ripped out pages from my maths book and wrote (forgive the spelling) L.W. SANTIN, F & F TOP SECRETT, KEP OUT!!! on the now upside-down back cover. I knew that I had been tasked with the job of cataloguing the flavours and feelings of my world.

For the next 20 years I filled book after book (kept in a secret box under my bed) with the flavours and feelings of my life. I would ponder the flavours and feelings of encounters with people and dutifully catalogue them. One day, a particularly odious interviewee that I had solicited information from happened to catch sight of the letters B.A.D. scribbled next to her name in large letters. I had been caught out and came clean, admitting that I was compiling a book of flavours and feelings, and that B.A.D. stood for Butterscotch Angel Delight. I remember my demonic delight as her face grew smugger at the thought of being likened to this sweet and fluffy food of the gods. What she didn't know was that just the smell of B.A.D. made me want to puke.

As a teenager the flavour of my catalogues changed. They were less matter of fact and more emotionally indulgent. Less time meant fewer words, and boys and bands were added to the endless entries of teachers, family and friends. Early adulthood saw boys replaced by men, school replaced by work and flavours and feelings muted and muffled as I threw ingredients into the fast-cooking pressure-cooker I called my life. The longer it cooked the worse it tasted, (something I tried to correct by adding more and more complicated and unlikely ingredients), and the further I got from an authentic recipe of me. It was only once the bottom caught and turned the whole soup acrid, that I found the courage to pick out the truth and sling the rest down the sink. I live by a far less complicated recipe now, where the simple nourishing ingredients of family and true friendships have brought about the healthful mind and body balance I had been searching for since that day in front of the mirror.

I still feel everything I taste, and taste everything I feel. Except these days, I apply that method to the recipes in my books and my flavour collection; each page, tube and jar contains a blend of the best natural flavours the world has to offer and they are all concocted with great care and love. I hope you will enjoy their transformational powers.

WHAT IS UMAMI AND HOW DO I USE IT?

The big misunderstanding is that because umami is a Japanese word used to describe 'savoury deliciousness' that umami must therefore be a Japanese or a Far Eastern concept. This is simply not so. To taste umami is like experiencing the feelings of love; the experiencing of umami is absolutely universal and does not, and cannot possibly belong to any single culture, but is shared, enjoyed and appreciated by all those in possession of a tongue.

Umami is one of the five basic tastes experienced by all humans when consuming food or drink, and it sits on our palates like the taste receptors for sweet, sour, bitter and salty. To understand umami is to understand how to transform your cooking and eating experience, and the reason I have spent so much time and effort delivering this powerful culinary secret to the domestic kitchen, is so that cooks of all levels can easily enjoy the magic of umami at home.

Although we may not all be aware of the term umami or the complex biochemistry of taste, human beings all over the world are all experiencing the raptures of 'savoury deliciousness' on a daily basis. Umami crosses cultural barriers and geographical boundaries, transcending age and gender. Even in sickness, scientists have proven that when all other tastes disappear from the patient's palate, umami deliciousness can often still be tasted.

How do you know if you have experienced umami? Umami fills the intensely savoury things that make you go 'mmmmm'. It is in that bit of caramelized chicken skin stuck to the bottom of the roasting tray, that salty anchovy that melts into the tomato on a pizza, or the irresistible, creamy combination of pancetta and Parmesan in a spaghetti carbonara.

Initially discovered just over 100 years ago, in 1908, by a Japanese scientist from Kyoto, Professor Kikunae Ikeda, the fifth taste was eventually accepted by Western scientists when it became clear that umami has its own taste receptors on the human tongue. The distinguishable savoury deliciousness of umami refers only to the intensely savoury taste imparted by glutamates (salts of the amino acid glutamic acid, found naturally bound with protein in foods) and five ribonucleotides, the building blocks of DNA, which occur naturally in many foods, including meat, fish, vegetables and dairy products.

Even though umami remained unrecognized and nameless for so long, it has been exploited to enhance and intensify the pleasure of food in every country and culture. From the fermented fish condiment liquamen used by the Ancient Greeks and Romans, to the much-loved cheeseburger-and-ketchup combination of today, the fifth taste has literally been an invisible delight on the tip of mankind's tongues since they had one.

I like to think of umami as the 'graphic equalizer' and 'amplifier' of all flavours. Fairly unremarkable on its own, this brothy phenomenon intensifies the taste of salt and sweet, and balances bitter and sour. It literally magnifies your dish, enhancing the flavours within individual ingredients and thus taking the entire dish to a whole new level of flavour.

My interest lies specifically in something called 'umami synergy'; this is the process whereby matching two very different ingredients recognized to be high in umami, such as tomatoes with minced beef, can increase the umami content eightfold. Apply this $1 + 1 = 8$ formula to a simple spaghetti Bolognese; when you begin by browning your mince and top the finished dish with Parmesan cheese, you create one of the most powerful flavour bombs known to man.

However, you don't need to be scientifically inclined to understand how to improve the flavour of your food by using umami – it is very easy indeed. This book teaches you how to create your own umami-packed flavour bombs using accessible everyday ingredients… with explosive results. So add some umami magic to your life today!

UMAMI-RICH FOOD

The table below is a pretty exhaustive, global list of sources of umami. I am in no way suggesting you need to go out and buy all of these in order to add some umami magic into your cooking. But if you take a look through the list below I'm sure there are plenty of ingredients you eat regularly anyway or already have in your store cupboard.

The graphic opposite shows the top 35 ingredients used in this book in terms of their relative umami content (measured in milligrams of free glutamate per 100 grams). It has been put together with the help of Dr Kumiko Ninomiya (the Umami 'Mama') from the Umami Information Center (http://www.umamiinfo.com).

FISH & SEAFOOD	FRUIT & VEGETABLES	MUSHROOMS	STORE CUPBOARD
Anchovies (fillets in oil)	Apple	Button	Anchovy paste
Bonito	Asparagus	Enoki	Aromat seasoning*
Bottarga	(green and white)	Porcini	Bragg Liquid Aminos
Caviar	Avocado	Shiitake	Colatura di alici
Cod	Bell pepper (green)	(fresh and dried)	Fish sauce
Crab	Broccoli	Truffles	Green tea
Herring	Cabbage		Kimchi paste
Lobster	Carrots		Maggi seasoning
Mackerel	Cauliflower	**DAIRY**	Miso paste
Oysters	Celery	Cabrales (goat's milk	MSG* (Accent flavour
Prawns/shrimp	Corn	blue cheese)	enhancer)
Salmon	Garlic	Camembert	Nutritional yeast flakes
Sardines	Ginger	Cheddar	Passata/strained
Scallops	Green peas	Danish blue	tomatoes
Sea bream	Grapefruit	Eggs (chicken's)	Sauerkraut
Squid	Kiwi fruit	Emmental	Seaweed (nori, wakame)
Tuna	Lettuce	Gouda	Shrimp paste
	Marrow	Gruyère de Comte	Soy sauce
	Onions	Milk (cow's)	Stock/bouillon
MEAT & POULTRY	Pear	Milk (goat's)	Sundried tomato paste
Beef	Potatoes	Parmigiano-Reggiano	Taste #5 Umami
Chicken	Spring onion/scallions	Roquefort	Collection (see p176)
Duck	Soy beans	Stilton	Tomato ketchup
Lamb	Strawberries		Tomato purée/paste
Pork	Sweet potatoes		Worcestershire sauce
Prosciutto crudo	Tomatoes		Yeast extracts (Marmite
(air-dried ham)	Tomatoes (sundried)		and Vegemite)
Salami			Walnuts

*see author's note (p175)

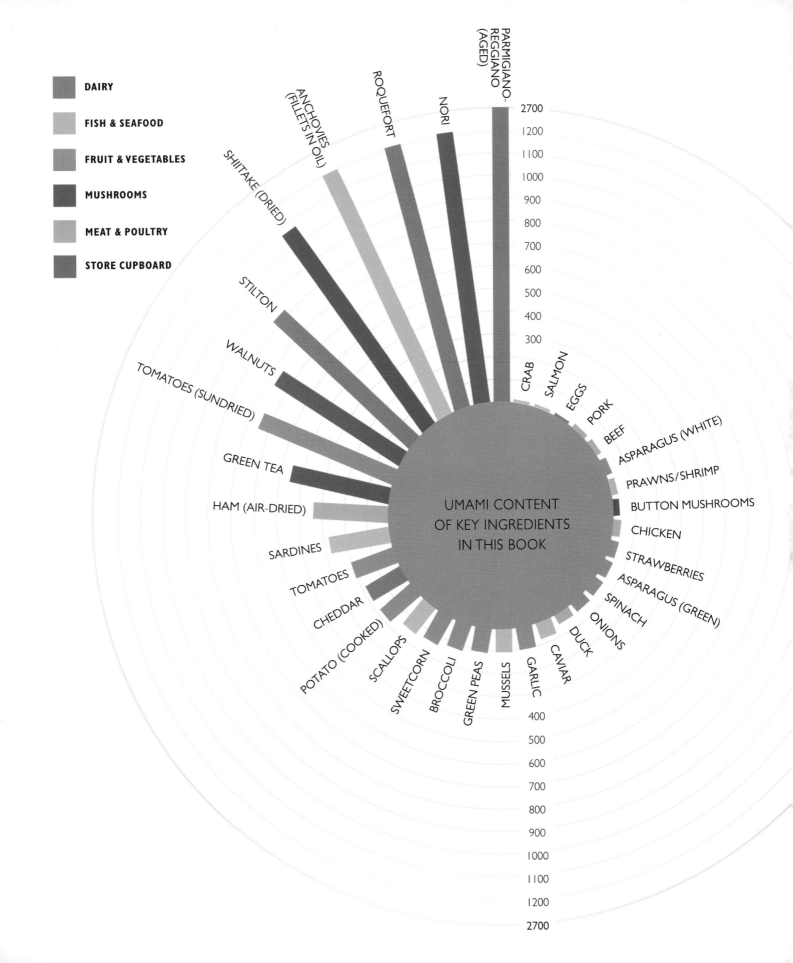

DAIRY

FISH & SEAFOOD

FRUIT & VEGETABLES

MUSHROOMS

MEAT & POULTRY

STORE CUPBOARD

PARMIGIANO-REGGIANO (AGED)

NORI

ROQUEFORT

ANCHOVIES (FILLETS IN OIL)

SHIITAKE (DRIED)

STILTON

WALNUTS

TOMATOES (SUNDRIED)

GREEN TEA

HAM (AIR-DRIED)

SARDINES

TOMATOES

CHEDDAR

POTATO (COOKED)

SCALLOPS

SWEETCORN

BROCCOLI

GREEN PEAS

MUSSELS

GARLIC

CAVIAR

DUCK

ONIONS

SPINACH

ASPARAGUS (GREEN)

STRAWBERRIES

CHICKEN

BUTTON MUSHROOMS

PRAWNS/SHRIMP

ASPARAGUS (WHITE)

BEEF

PORK

EGGS

SALMON

CRAB

UMAMI CONTENT
OF KEY INGREDIENTS
IN THIS BOOK

2700
1200
1100
1000
900
800
700
600
500
400
300

400
500
600
700
800
900
1000
1100
1200
2700

CONTENTS
WHAT DO YOU FEEL LIKE COOKING?

When we think about what or where to eat we usually say something like 'what do you feel like eating?' The pursuit of deliciousness is all about doing what you feel like with maximum flavour. Use the flavours and feelings below to match your food to your mood or to change your mood with your food; both are equally possible. Use the golden bookmark to track the flavours and feelings in your world, taking time to contemplate what you felt like last time you picked this book up and what you feel like now. Monitor the flavours and feelings of your life to ensure that whatever the feeling, you will ultimately be lead to deliciousness…

FRESH & UPLIFTING

Delicious for breakfast with thick Greek yogurt, mango, avocado, and even a handful of chopped coriander/cilantro and a little bit of extra virgin olive oil, this granola is equally fabulous on soups, salads and vegetables. Where I seem to eat it the most, however, is from the bottom of my handbag after the granola spills out of the container I've stored it in. It's for this reason that my affectionate nickname for this recipe is 'handbag heaven'!

SAVOURY GRANOLA

90 g/1 cup rolled oats
60 g/½ cup pistachios, shelled
60 g/½ cup walnuts, roughly quartered
60 g/7 tablespoons sunflower seeds
40 g/5 tablespoons sesame seeds
½ tablespoon fennel seeds
½ tablespoon coriander seeds
20 g/¾ oz cacao nibs
½ teaspoon cayenne pepper
1 teaspoon sea salt flakes
2 rosemary sprigs, leaves only, roughly chopped
1 tablespoon freshly grated lemon zest
4 tablespoons olive oil
1 tablespoons maple syrup
1 tablespoon soy sauce
1 large egg white, lightly beaten

SERVES 2–3 (OR 4–6 HANDBAG HANDFULS)

Preheat the oven to 180°C (360°F) Gas 4.

Combine the oats, nuts, seeds and cacao nibs in a large bowl. Sprinkle over the cayenne pepper, salt, rosemary and lemon zest and give it a good mix.

Add the olive oil, maple syrup, soy sauce, and mix thoroughly again.

Finally mix in the beaten egg white and combine.

Spread the mixture in a thin layer on a non-stick baking sheet.

Bake for 20–25 minutes, stirring a couple of times, until just nicely golden brown. Keep a close eye on the mixture as the seeds can burn very quickly.

Allow the granola to cool and then serve with a good dollop of Greek yogurt. The granola will keep for two weeks in a sealed plastic container.

This vibrant and earthy green tea dressing is packed with antioxidants and healthful flavours. To taste the real benefits of this vital vinaigrette, try to use a good cold-pressed extra virgin olive oil. I often replace half of the olive oil with an omega 3-6-9 oil from a health-food shop and add a spoonful of raw cacao nibs with the herbs. The umami secret in this recipe is the mixing of all five basic tastes; sweet, sour, bitter and salty meld with the green tea to really bring out the umami in the asparagus.

QUINOA & ASPARAGUS SALAD WITH MATCHA LEMON DRESSING

SALAD

100 g/½ cup black or red quinoa (I prefer black because it is the crunchiest)

sea salt

2 tablespoons olive oil

a bunch of asparagus spears, woody ends cut off

4 oranges

2 large avocados

1 large red onion, finely sliced

handful of mint, roughly chopped

handful of basil, roughly chopped

4 large handfuls rocket/arugula leaves

DRESSING

1 garlic clove, crushed

freshly squeezed juice of 1 lemon

½ teaspoon matcha green tea

pinch of wasabi paste or powder to taste (optional)

sea salt and freshly ground black pepper

7 tablespoons extra virgin olive oil

TO SERVE

1 handful toasted pumpkin seeds

SERVES 4

Rinse the quinoa in cold water and then cook in a large saucepan of salted boiling water for about 12–20 minutes (depending on the colour) until the grains become soft but still have some bite.

Meanwhile, make the dressing by combining all the ingredients apart from the oil in a bowl and then whisk in the oil. Season to taste and set aside.

Once the quinoa is cooked, drain, stir through a little olive oil to stop it from sticking together and set aside to cool.

Steam or boil the asparagus until cooked and the stalks are al dente. Remove from the heat, drain and refresh under cold running water to fix the colour and set aside. Slice each stalk on the diagonal into thumb-length spears.

With a sharp knife cut down the sides of the oranges to remove the skin and pith and slice the orange into 1 cm/½ in. discs. Save any juice from the oranges to add to your dressing.

Peel and cut the avocados into large chunks.

Put all the salad ingredients, including the herbs and rocket/arugula, into a large serving dish and toss together.

To serve, pour the dressing (adding any reserved orange juice first) onto the salad and combine well.

Serve with a scattering of toasted pumpkin seeds.

A perfect example of culinary alchemy, the humble ingredients tomato, basil, salt and oil transform into something far more precious than the sum of each of their simple parts. I was once at a dinner and we were all asked if we had a last meal on earth what would it be. This dish was mine, because when I taste this magical combination, it is clear to me that the universe is greater than our simple lives: it is the sum of us all that has the potential to turn life into gold.

RIPE BEEF TOMATO & BASIL ALCHEMY

4 large and perfectly ripe heirloom beef tomatoes
high-quality extra virgin olive oil
sea salt flakes and freshly ground black pepper
freshly squeezed juice of 1 lemon
1 handful fresh basil leaves, torn
rustic crusty white bread, to serve

SERVES 2

Wash the tomatoes and then cut them in slices.

Drizzle over a good glug of olive oil and season with salt and pepper and a squeeze of lemon juice.

Top with torn basil leaves.

Serve with lovely crusty white bread – perfect for mopping up those umami-packed juices!

A delicate and tasty carpaccio, once you have decided that life's not too short to thinly slice a mushroom… Note that I have stressed to use extra virgin olive oil to dress and just a couple of drops of truffle oil, which I think is best used really sparingly.

CHESTNUT MUSHROOM CARPACCIO WITH PECORINO & TRUFFLE OIL

8 large chestnut mushrooms
6 Brussels sprouts, finely
** shredded**
small handful flat-leaf
** parsley, roughly chopped**
Pecorino cheese shavings
extra virgin olive oil
truffle oil
freshly squeezed lemon
** juice (optional)**

SERVES 2

Slice the mushrooms as thinly as possible using a very sharp knife.

Arrange the mushroom slices on a large serving plate and top with the shredded sprouts.

Season with salt and pepper, sprinkle with parsley, Pecorino cheese shavings and drizzle with extra virgin olive oil and a few drops of truffle oil. If you wish, add a very light squeeze of lemon, but I prefer it without.

ARTICHOKE RAVIGOTE

This dish is perfect as a spring or summer starter or as a light meal in itself. The first time I ever tasted this version of a ravigote sauce (a classic French vinegar sauce with onion/shallot, capers and herbs) was at a family lunch in London; simple and so sophisticated, it is packed with umami from the eggs and full of the promise of spring. This sauce is fantastic as a dip for crudités.

6 globe artichokes
freshly squeezed juice of
** 1 lemon**
½ tablespoon fine salt
1 teaspoon black
** peppercorns**
3 bay leaves
handful of fresh flat-leaf
** parsley**

RAVIGOTE-STYLE SAUCE
150 g/5½ oz. fresh flat-leaf
** parsley**
3 hard-boiled eggs
200 g/7 oz. drained capers
350 ml/1½ cups extra virgin
** olive oil**
2 tablespoons white wine
** vinegar**
freshly ground black pepper

SERVES 6

Prepare each artichoke by trimming off the top, removing any woody outer leaves, cutting off the stalk and rinsing.

Put the artichokes in a large stainless steel pan, cover with cold water, and add the lemon juice, salt, peppercorns and herbs. Cover with a lid and bring to the boil. Once boiling, turn down to a simmer, cover partially and leave to simmer for 30–40 minutes until they are cooked. You know they are done when you can easily pull a leaf out 3–4 leaves down from the top.

Remove the artichokes from the pan and drain upside-down in a colander.

To make the sauce, first blitz the parsley in a food processor. Then add the eggs and pulse again. Then add the capers and blitz again. Pour in the olive oil and white wine vinegar, season to taste with pepper and blitz one more time.

Divide the sauce between 6 small bowls or ramekins and give one to each person alongside a globe artichoke.

SICILIAN POTATO SALAD

The perfect accompaniment to any summer BBQ, this flavourful potato salad is a departure from traditional mayo-based salads and visually very inviting. It is really important to use a good-quality olive oil, as the secret to the recipe lies in the quality of the ingredients and how the hot potatoes unlock these fresh aromatics. As a quick side dish, I often leave out the other aromatics and simply dress hot boiled potatoes with olive oil, squashed garlic, plenty of parsley and salt and pepper – it never fails!

1 kg/2 lbs. 3 oz. potatoes
** (the yellow waxy type**
** work best), peeled and**
** cut into bite-sized chunks**
400 g/2¼ cups cherry
** tomatoes, halved**
3 garlic cloves, squashed
** and cut in half**
7–9 anchovy fillets, finely
** chopped**
6 celery stalks with leaves,
** chopped into 1.5-cm/**
** ½-in. pieces**
4 tablespoons pickled
** capers, drained**
1 red onion, thinly sliced

4 spring onions/scallions,
** thinly sliced**
100 g/1 cup stoned/pitted
** mixed olives**
1 large handful fresh basil,
** torn**
1 large handful fresh
** flat-leaf parsley, finely**
** chopped**
finely grated zest of
** 1 lemon**
extra virgin olive oil
sea salt and freshly ground
** black pepper, to taste**

SERVES 4–6

Put the potatoes in a large pan of salted water and bring to the boil. Once boiling cook until tender in the centre but still firm, because you do not want them crumbling.

Put all the other salad ingredients in a large bowl with a good glug of extra virgin olive oil and toss gently.

Drain the potatoes and shake gently to ensure all the moisture has gone. Add the hot potatoes to the oil and salad mixture and dress with more extra virgin olive oil and salt and pepper to taste. Serve immediately.

Brilliant for a casually sophisticated dinner party, you can also use this versatile marinade for fish fillets. You will win over your guests with the sweet rice and super-savoury but super-light fish. Serve with a crisp green salad.

THAI-STEAMED SNAPPER WITH STICKY COCONUT JASMINE RICE

1 whole red snapper or other whole sustainable* white fish, about 2 kg/4½ lbs., descaled, gutted and cleaned

4 limes (1 sliced)

1 bunch fresh coriander/cilantro

1 bunch of spring onions/scallions, topped and sliced (reserve tops for stuffing fish)

1 sweet potato, diced into thumbnail-sized pieces

2.5-cm/1-in. piece of fresh ginger, sliced

5 garlic cloves, peeled

3 lemongrass stalks, outer skin removed and roughly chopped

2 red chillies/chiles, deseeded (keep the seeds of half a chilli/chile only)

3 tablespoons toasted sesame oil

4 tablespoons fish sauce

3 tablespoons soy sauce

1 tablespoon brown sugar or palm sugar

STICKY COCONUT JASMINE RICE

200 g/1 cup plus 2 tablespoons sticky rice

400-ml/14-oz. can coconut milk

½ teaspoon salt

1 teaspoon caster/granulated sugar

½ teaspoon jasmine green tea (optional)

50 g/⅔ cup desiccated/dried shredded coconut

SERVES 4

see author's note on p175

Preheat the oven to 200°C (400°F) Gas 6.

Cut a piece of wide baking parchment twice the length of your fish. Fold the parchment in half and then open it, placing one half on a baking tray. Put the fish on the diagonal on the piece of parchment on the baking tray.

Make slashes in the fish on the diagonal through the skin down to the bone on both sides. Stuff the cavity with a few slices of lime, half the coriander/cilantro and the tops of the spring onions/scallions. Scatter sweet potato cubes and spring onion/scallion chunks around the fish.

In a food processor, combine the rest of the coriander/cilantro, ginger, garlic, lemongrass and chilli/chile and blitz into a paste. Add the sesame oil, fish sauce, soy sauce, sugar and the juice of the remaining 3 limes and blitz again.

Rub this marinade all over the fish and fold the other half of parchment over the fish and wrap the edges over to close tightly (you can use a stapler if you need to but don't forget they are there!)

Cook in the preheated oven for 25–30 minutes or until the fish is cooked. To test if the fish is cooked, remove from the oven and take a peek inside a corner of the parcel, but be careful because the steam will escape. If the eye of the fish has turned white, this means your fish is cooked.

While the fish is in the oven, make the rice. Put the rice in a non-stick medium saucepan (that has a lid), and add the coconut milk, salt, sugar and jasmine tea (if using). Place over a medium heat and bring to the boil. Once boiling, put the lid on the pan and turn the heat down to low. Leave to cook for 15–20 minutes on a really low heat – do not be tempted stir or to lift the lid off before 15 minutes as this will let the steam escape. Turn the heat off and leave the rice until ready to serve.

Once the fish is cooked, open the parcel and serve large chunks of fish on the creamy, sticky rice topped with a large spoonful of the cooking juices – that is where most of the umami is.

WRINKLED BEANS

This delicious recipe first featured in my book *Flash Cooking*. It is a firm favourite with flavour enthusiasts – particularly those searching for the perfect umami hit.

2 tablespoons sesame oil

1 tablespoon soy sauce, plus an extra 2 splashes

2.5-cm/1-in. piece fresh ginger root, grated

3–4 garlic cloves, finely chopped or crushed

7 sundried tomatoes in oil, drained and finely chopped

1 lemongrass stalk, tough outer leaves removed and stalk cut lengthways into 4 pieces

1 tablespoon Taste #5 Umami Bomb/Paste Original Recipe, or yeast extract, such as **Marmite** or **Vegemite**

400 g/14 oz. fine green/string beans, trimmed

2 splashes fish sauce

2 splashes soy sauce

furikake (dry Japanese seasoning) or toasted sesame seeds, to serve

SERVES 4–6 AS A SIDE

Put 1 tablespoon of the sesame oil, the tablespoon of soy sauce, ginger, garlic, sun-dried tomatoes, lemongrass and Umami Bomb/Paste (or yeast extract) into a food processor and blitz until it becomes a rough paste.

Heat a wok until it is smoking hot, then add the other tablespoon of sesame oil and the blended paste and stir-fry for 1–2 minutes until fragrant.

Add the beans and stir-fry until they are coated with all the paste.

Add the fish sauce, extra soy sauce and a splash of water, continuing to stir. As the water evaporates keep adding additional splashes of water until the beans are softened and begin to wrinkle, but are still al dente.

Serve with a sprinkle of furikake or toasted sesame seeds.

WHITE MISO & TAHINI-ROASTED VEGETABLES

A super-quick and healthy midweek supper, served with a spicy, tangy harissa yogurt.

1 kg/2 lbs. 3 oz. roasting vegetables (onions and root vegetables or Mediterranean vegetables) cut into 4–5-cm/1½–2-in. pieces

2 heads of garlic with the top sliced off

2 tablespoons olive oil

3 fresh thyme sprigs or 1 teaspoon dried thyme

1 teaspoon dried oregano

sea salt and freshly ground black pepper

1 handful of toasted cashew nuts, to serve

ROASTING SAUCE

50 g/1 heaped tablespoon white miso

60 g/¼ cup tahini

½ tablespoon pomegranate molasses

½ teaspoon ground cumin

1 teaspoon cumin seeds

1 tablespoon olive oil

good grinding of freshly ground black pepper

HARISSA YOGURT

3 tablespoons Greek-style yogurt

1 teaspoon rose harissa paste

1 tablespoon chopped fresh mint leaves

grated zest of 1 lemon and a squeeze of juice

SERVES 4

Preheat the oven to 220°C (425°F) Gas 7.

Place the vegetables and garlic in a non-stick baking tray. Toss them in the olive oil, sprinkle with thyme and oregano and season with salt and pepper, giving them a good mix to ensure they are all coated in the oil. Make sure there is space between them, otherwise they will steam rather than roast. Place in the preheated oven for approximately 35–40 minutes. Halfway through cooking, toss carefully to ensure even colour.

Whisk the roasting sauce ingredients together with 100 ml/ 7 tablespoons of boiling water. The mixture should be the consistency of a drop scone batter.

Once the vegetables have been roasting for around 30–35 minutes, pour over the sauce and cook for 5 more minutes.

Make the harissa yogurt by simply combining the ingredients.

Remove the vegetables from the oven, scatter with cashew nuts and serve with the yogurt.

Traditionally, borscht is made with beet(root) and beef, but replacing the beef with the satisfying brothiness of miso showcases the power of umami. I like to use Hikari miso, which is available worldwide and is still made in Japan to the exacting standards of this traditional family business. You'll find that you won't even miss the meat in this recipe. I've left this soup quite dense as I am a big fan of a meal in a bowl. You can always add a little more stock or water if you like it more brothy and less stewy.

MISO BORSCHT WITH ORANGE & LEMON-JUNIPER GREMOLATA

30 g/1 cup dried porcini mushrooms
2 tablespoons olive oil
300 g/4½ cups chestnut mushrooms, sliced
1 large onion, cut into 1-cm/½-in chunks
1 kg/2 lbs. 3 oz. beet(root), peeled and cut into 1-cm/½-in chunks
2 carrots, cut into 1-cm/½-in chunks
1 leek, cut into 1-cm/½-in chunks
3 garlic cloves, finely chopped
½ small white cabbage, cored and shredded
500 g/1 lb. 2 oz. potatoes, cut into 1-cm/½-in chunks
1 tablespoon brown miso paste
3 tablespoons tomato purée/paste
1 bunch dill, finely chopped

1 bunch flat-leaf parsley, finely chopped
1 tablespoon runny honey
½ teaspoon chilli/hot red pepper flakes
125 ml/½ cup cider vinegar
sea salt and freshly ground black pepper

TO SERVE
sour cream
fresh flat-leaf parsley, finely chopped

ORANGE & LEMON JUNIPER GREMOLATA
zest of 1 lemon, finely chopped
zest of 1 orange, finely chopped
handful of fresh flat-leaf parsley, finely chopped
5 juniper berries (ground using a pestle and mortar)

SERVES 6–8

Place the dried mushrooms in a bowl and cover in boiling water to rehydrate for around 20 minutes. When they are plump and the liquid is dark, remove them and reserve the liquid.

Heat the oil over a medium heat in a large heavy-based saucepan. Add the fresh mushrooms and onion and sauté until they begin to soften.

Add the beet(root), carrots, leek, garlic, 2 litres/quarts water and strain in the mushroom soaking liquid to avoid adding the gritty residue at the bottom of the bowl.

Bring to the boil, then lower the heat and simmer for 5 minutes. Stir in the cabbage, potatoes and rehydrated mushrooms.

Add the miso paste and tomato purée/paste and return to the boil. Lower the heat and simmer until all the vegetables are cooked but with an al dente bite.

Remove the borscht from the heat. Stir in the dill, parsley, honey, chilli/hot red pepper flakes and vinegar and season with salt and pepper to taste (this may not be necessary).

To make the gremolata simply mix all ingredients together in a bowl.

Serve with a dollop of sour cream, fresh parsley and a sprinkle of gremolata.

This rub is a beautiful thing, but with good-quality steak and a drizzle of good green extra virgin olive oil, it is ridiculously sublime. For extra umami add a couple of Portobello mushrooms to the dish – just sprinkle them with a little rub and pan-fry them with the steaks. This rub recipe makes more than you need for 2 steaks but I like to store the excess in a tightly sealed jar and use on other meats and fish.

UMAMI STEAK TAGLIATA

2 steaks (rib-eye,
   sirloin/New York strip
   or fillet/filet mignon)
extra virgin olive oil,
   for drizzling

GARLIC PESTO
2 large garlic cloves
leaves from 2 sprigs
   of rosemary
5 black peppercorns
extra virgin olive oil
good pinch of salt

UMAMI RUB
(makes 120 g/4 oz.)
1 tablespoon dried
   mushrooms (shiitake,
   porcini or a mix;
   you will need about
   a handful to make
   a tablespoon)
2 tablespoons sea salt
1 tablespoon brown
   sugar
1 tablespoon smoked
   paprika
1 tablespoon dried
   oregano
2 teaspoons ground
   cumin
2 teaspoons garlic
   powder
1 teaspoon ground black
   pepper
½ teaspoon cayenne
   pepper (or to taste)

SERVES 2

Using a pestle and mortar, pound together the garlic, rosemary, black peppercorns and salt to a chunky pesto consistency. Add just enough oil to form a loose pesto and set aside.

Next make the rub. Start by grinding the dried mushrooms to a powder in either a spice grinder or a coffee grinder.

Combine all the rub ingredients in a bowl until well mixed through.

Generously rub each steak all over with about a tablespoon of the rub. Once they are well coated, place the steaks on a plate and drizzle with some of the garlic pesto keeping the rest aside. If time permits, cover the steaks in clingfilm/plastic wrap and leave them for about 20–30 minutes to come to room temperature.

Preheat a frying pan/skillet on a medium-high heat. Once hot, cook the steaks to your liking.

Once cooked, remove the steaks from the pan and leave to rest for a minute or so in a warm place. Slice diagonally with a sharp knife.

Serve on warmed plates topped with any pan juices, an extra spoonful of the garlic pesto and a good drizzle of extra virgin olive oil.

This is a very popular dish at my restaurant Santini in London's Belgravia, and features a really fresh and clean dressing – something of a departure from the classic mayo carpaccio dressing. If I am in a hurry I replace the raw beef with either sliced rare roast beef from the deli counter or a good, thinly sliced bresaola.

BEEF CARPACCIO

500 g/1 lb. 2 oz. middle-cut beef fillet/filet mignon or bresaola
sea salt and freshly ground black pepper
8–9 cherry tomatoes, halved
1 bunch (around 100 g/3½ oz.) rocket/arugula leaves
50 g/⅔ cup Parmesan cheese shavings
extra virgin olive oil
squeeze of lemon juice

SERVES 4

If you're using beef fillet/filet mignon and not bresaola, wrap the beef in clingfilm/plastic wrap and put in the freezer for 1 hour to firm up.

Slice the firmed-up beef into thin rounds about 0.25 cm/⅛ in. thick. You can also cut slightly thicker pieces, then put them between two sheets of clingfilm/plastic wrap and flatten with a rolling pin.

Cover a chilled plate with the beef or bresaola slices. If not serving immediately (it is much better if you do), cover each plate with clingfilm/plastic wrap and refrigerate to avoid the meat discolouring.

To serve, season with salt and pepper (only pepper if using bresaola), and scatter the tomatoes and rocket/arugula on top of the beef. Top with shavings of Parmesan cheese and drizzle over olive oil and lemon juice.

From left: Buckwheat & Enoki
Mushroom Salad, Brown Rice & Tuna
Salad and Kimchi Coleslaw.

Usually fermented in a laundry cupboard for days, this version of kimchi does not need fermenting – it is a quick and crunchy coleslaw variant of the Korean speciality. Clearly it lacks the healthful properties of fermented foods but it is packed with flavourful vitamins all the same. A great side with all your grills.

Once you have chopped all the ingredients, all you have to do to make this dish is pour over the hot rice and all the flavours come alive. I like to make this in bulk as it keeps its bite well in the fridge for a couple of days and is easy for packed lunches or quick summer suppers.

KIMCHI COLESLAW

½ red cabbage, shredded
½ white cabbage, shredded
2 fennel bulbs, shredded
3 carrots, grated
10 radishes, sliced thinly
    into rounds
2 Granny Smith apples,
    grated
150 g/1 cup plump raisins
100 g/⅔ cup walnut halves,
    lightly toasted in a pan

KIMCHI DRESSING
5 tablespoons sesame oil
3 tablespoons fish sauce
freshly squeezed juice of
    1½ lemons
large, thumb-sized piece
    of ginger, grated
3 garlic cloves, crushed
1½ teaspoons runny honey
a pinch of cayenne pepper
    (or to taste)

SERVES 6

Place the vegetables, apples, raisins and walnuts in a large bowl.

Whisk together all the dressing ingredients until well combined. Pour it over the other ingredients and give everything a good mix to ensure that the dressing coats all the ingredients well.

Cover and leave in the fridge for 2–3 hours before serving.

BROWN RICE & TUNA SALAD

200 g/2 scant cups brown
    short-grain rice
½ red onion, finely chopped
2 garlic cloves, squashed
    and cut in half
1 teaspoon rose harissa or
    chilli paste
freshly squeezed juice and
    rind of 1 lemon
300 g/2 cups cherry
    tomatoes, quartered
handful of fresh mint, finely
    chopped

handful of fresh flat-leaf
    parsley, finely chopped
190-g/6¾-oz. jar of tuna
    fillets or alternatively
    200-g/7-oz. can tuna steak
1–2 tablespoons Taste #5
    Umami Bomb/Paste
    Original Recipe or
    sundried tomato paste
good glug of extra virgin
    olive oil
sea salt and freshly ground
    black pepper

SERVES 4–6

Cook the rice as per the packet instructions but make sure it still has bite i.e. still a little al dente. Drain and set aside for 5 minutes to cool while you prepare the other ingredients.

Put all the other ingredients in a large bowl. When the rice has cooled slightly, pour it over the other ingredients and toss it all together to combine the flavours. Season to taste.

I call enoki mushrooms 'catwalk' mushrooms, because their physical elegance and subtle flavour is all that you might expect to see in a modern art gallery or on a contemporary runway. They are truly a thing of wonder and this clean salad is the perfect backdrop for their understated elegance. For the ultimate in refined deliciousness, replace the salad leaves with steamed white asparagus when in season.

BUCKWHEAT & ENOKI MUSHROOM SALAD

175 g/1 cup raw buckwheat groats

8 spring onions/scallions, thinly sliced

1 bunch of chives finely snipped or fresh red shiso leaves (hard to find but delicious!)

400 g/6 cups enoki mushrooms (firm and white, avoid slimy or brownish stalks, unless using golden enoki which should also be firm and not slimy)

4 generous handfuls mixed salad leaves (lamb's lettuce works best), or 8 white asparagus spears, steamed

2 tablespoons furikake (dry Japanese seasoning) or toasted sesame seeds

UMAMI VINAIGRETTE

2 tablespoons soy sauce

2 tablespoons toasted sesame oil

2 teaspoons rice vinegar

freshly squeezed juice of 2 limes

2.5-cm/1-in. piece of fresh ginger, finely grated

2–3 teaspoons runny honey (or to taste)

good pinch cayenne pepper (or to taste)

SERVES 2

Rinse the buckwheat before cooking. Place buckwheat into a saucepan with 500 ml/2 cups water and a good pinch of salt. Bring to a boil and turn down to a simmer. Cook until al dente, drain if necessary and then refresh under cold water to get rid of any starchiness. Set aside to cool.

Combine the vinaigrette ingredients in a large mixing bowl and whisk together. Add the spring onion/scallion and chives and leave to sit for 10 minutes if you have time.

Place the mushrooms and buckwheat in a bowl and add two-thirds of the vinaigrette. Gently combine until all the ingredients are coated.

Place a handful of salad leaves or the steamed asparagus on each plate and top with the buckwheat mushroom mixture.

Sprinkle about half a teaspoon of furikake or toasted sesame seeds on each plate and drizzle with the remaining dressing.

SPAGHETTI ALLA PUTTANESCA

High heels and lipstick to serve. Yes, you too boys!!

150 ml/⅔ cup olive oil

4 garlic cloves, thinly sliced

2 fresh red chillies/chiles, deseeded and finely chopped, or ½ teaspoon chilli/hot red pepper flakes

600 g/4 cups fresh cherry tomatoes, halved lengthways

4 tablespoons drained and roughly chopped stoned/pitted black olives in olive oil (choose Kalamata or Taggiasche)

2 tablespoons capers, drained

5 anchovies in oil, drained and roughly chopped

handful of basil leaves, torn

freshly ground black pepper

400 g/3½ oz. dried spaghetti

zest of 1 lemon

SERVES 4

Heat the oil in a heavy-based saucepan and sauté the garlic and chillies/chiles until the garlic begins to colour.

Stir in all the other ingredients, except the lemon zest and season with black pepper (the olives, capers and anchovies will probably make it salty enough).

Allow to simmer gently on a low heat for about 10–15 minutes, or until the tomatoes begin to break down. If the tomatoes are too acidic, balance with a pinch of sugar.

Cook the spaghetti in plenty of salted boiling water until al dente.

Place the sauce in a large serving bowl with lemon zest, drain the pasta and add to the sauce. Toss and serve.

CITRUS POPCORN CEVICHE

In ceviche, the raw fish is 'cooked' using the acidic juices from citrus fruits rather than heat. It is important to keep the acidity levels high; otherwise there will be no 'cooking' and your ceviche will be slimy. Don't be tempted to prepare ceviche too far in advance, as the acid will continue to break down the protein in the fish and it will lose its texture.

2 large oranges – zest and juice of 1 orange and the flesh of the other

500 g/1 lb. 2 oz. skinned, boneless fresh fish (cod, salmon, sole, tilapia, tuna, scallops or any lean white fish are ideal)

freshly squeezed juice of 3 lemons

freshly squeezed juice of 3 limes

1 garlic clove, crushed

1 fresh red chilli/chile pepper, finely chopped (half deseeded for less heat)

handful of coriander/ cilantro, finely chopped

handful of flat-leaf parsley, finely chopped

salt flakes and freshly ground black pepper

400 g/2⅓ cups cherry tomatoes, cut into quarters

½ cucumber, diced

1–2 tablespoons fish sauce, to taste

2 bunches of spring onions/scallions, thinly sliced

TO SERVE

2 handfuls of popped corn (optional)

1 little gem lettuce

SERVES 4

Peel and slice one of the oranges into 0.5-cm/¼-in. discs and set aside.

Combine all the ingredients except the spring onion/scallion and orange slices and mix thoroughly.

Place the spring onion/scallion and orange slices on the top of the mixture, cover and refrigerate for 2–3 hours.

When you are ready to serve, remove from the fridge, scatter with the popcorn (if using) and give it all a good stir. Scoop up the ceviche with the little gem lettuce.

PUMPKIN SEED, PARSLEY & PARMESAN SCALLOPS

It is worth asking your fishmonger for some scallop shells (they can be washed and re-used) as they do make the serving of this dish all the more special. The idea came from the traditional way we serve scallops in Venice, which is with a little garlic, parsley and breadcrumbs. However, this mix is greener and lighter and any leftover crumb can be used on fish fillets or sprinkled over salads and soups.

75 g/½ cup pumpkin seeds

25 g/1 oz. fresh flat-leaf parsley

zest of 1 lemon

50 g/½ cup Parmesan cheese, cut into chunks

1 garlic clove

salt and freshly ground black pepper, to taste

16 king scallops (coral on), plus 8 scallop shells, for serving

1 lemon

extra virgin olive oil

SERVES 4

Preheat oven to 180°C (350°F) Gas 4.

Place the pumpkin seeds, parsley, lemon zest, Parmesan cheese and garlic in a food processor and pulse until it resembles coarse breadcrumbs. Season with salt and pepper to taste.

Place 2 scallops in each shell, season with a little salt and pepper and top each shell with 3 teaspoons of the crumb mixture, leaving the orange coral uncovered.

Place the shells on a baking tray and drizzle each one with a little extra virgin olive oil and a squeeze of lemon.

Bake in the preheated oven for 10–15 minutes until the scallops firm up and the crust begins to colour.

It is really worth taking the time one Saturday morning to make a batch of these super helpful, super healthful flavour bombs. Make them ahead and keep them in a resealable bag in the freezer, so you can just get home from work and let the cubes do the work for you. You can make a simple steam-fry supper for one with just a single cube and some vegetables. The big umami hit in this recipe comes from the Bragg Liquid Aminos.

GLASS NOODLE, SHIITAKE & VEGETABLE STEAM-FRY

FOR STIR-FRYING

200 g/7 oz. Korean glass noodles (made from sweet potato) or other glass noodles

1 tablespoon sesame oil, plus extra for loosening

300 g/10½ oz. shiitake mushrooms, sliced

300 g/10½ oz. mixed stir-fry vegetables, chopped

3 flavour bomb cubes (see right)

Bragg Liquid Aminos or a good squeeze of Taste #5 Umami Bomb/Paste (Vegetarian Garlic)

toasted mixed seeds

FLAVOUR BOMBS

400 g/14 oz. fresh ginger, chopped

3 whole heads of garlic cloves, peeled

3 red chillies/chiles, 2 deseeded

2 bunches spring onions/scallions, trimmed and chopped

1 large bunch coriander/cilantro

1 small bunch of Thai basil

1 bunch of flat-leaf parsley

2 teaspoons turmeric powder

freshly squeezed juice and zest of 3 limes

SERVES 2

To make the flavour bombs, place all the ingredients into a food processor and pulse until a smooth paste is formed, adding splashes of water as needed to loosen it to a smooth paste.

Fill ice-cube trays with paste leaving a little space as they will expand when they freeze. If you do not want to use trays you can freeze blobs in squares of tightly wrapped clingfilm/plastic wrap.

Once frozen, tip all the cubes into a resealable plastic bag so you have them to hand as and when you need them.

Cook the glass noodles in a large pan of boiling water for around 5 minutes; they should still be al dente. Drain and rinse with cold water, return them to the pan and mix with a splash of sesame oil to stop them from sticking together.

When ready to steam-fry, heat the tablespoon of sesame oil in a wok or frying pan/skillet and fry the flavour bomb cubes until fragrant (taking care not to burn them). Add the mushrooms and vegetables and a splash of water from the kettle and steam fry until cooked but al dente.

Add the noodles and season with Bragg Liquid Aminos or Umami Bomb/Paste and some toasted mixed seeds.

Enjoy how virtuous this healthful umami mix makes you feel!

The smoky chipotle and the aromatic orange zest give this traditional Bourguignon base a little extra *je ne sais quoi*. Serve with creamy mashed potatoes.

SMOKY RED WINE SHORT RIBS

4 tablespoons olive oil

1.5–2 kg/3¼–4½ lbs. beef short ribs

salt and freshly ground black pepper

75 g/2½ oz. (approx. 5 slices) prosciutto, finely chopped

1 large Spanish onion, finely chopped

2 carrots, finely chopped

2 celery stalks, finely chopped

3 garlic cloves, peeled and finely chopped

1 bottle of medium-quality full-bodied red wine

1 large tablespoon double concentrated tomato purée/paste

3 anchovies in oil, drained

1 large strip of orange peel

500 ml/2 cups beef stock

1 rosemary sprig

1 thyme sprig

2 bay leaves

1 dried chipotle chilli (deseeded or with half the seeds left in if you like it hot)

SERVES 6–8

Preheat the oven to 160°C (325°F) Gas 3.

Heat the oil over a medium/high heat in a large heavy-based ovenproof saucepan with a lid. Add the ribs and brown on all sides. Once well browned, remove the ribs, set aside and season.

Turn the heat down to low-medium and, in the same pan, sauté the prosciutto until it begins to crisp.

Add the onion, carrots, celery and garlic, and cook until the onions are glassy. Deglaze the pot with one glass of wine, scraping the bottom of the pan with a wooden spoon to make sure that you incorporate all the caramelized cooking juices – a great source of umami.

When the wine has almost evaporated, add the rest of the wine, tomato purée/paste, anchovies, orange peel, stock, rosemary, thyme, bay leaves and chipotle chilli.

Stir well and add the ribs back to the pan along with any juices, bring to the boil then transfer to the preheated oven with the lid tightly on, for 2½ hours, or until the meat is tender. Turn occasionally during cooking to make sure all sides get immersed in the sauce. If at the end of cooking, your sauce is too thin, remove the meat and reduce the sauce over a low heat with the lid off until you have the thick consistency you prefer.

NOTE: If the ribs are very fatty, I like to trim some of the fat off before searing them.

Children of all ages love this tasty and nourishing midweek supper. For those in a hurry, it is also super-quick to make, especially if you buy your cheese already grated.

BACON & CHERRY TOMATO CAULIFLOWER CHEESE

CAULIFLOWER CHEESE
1 cauliflower
sea salt and freshly ground
  black pepper
12 rashers/slices
  streaky/fatty bacon
250 g/1½ cups cherry
  tomatoes
1 handful grated/shredded
  Cheddar cheese

CHEESE SAUCE
575 ml/2½ cups milk
50 g/⅓ cup plain/
  all-purpose flour
60 g/4 tablespoons butter
1 teaspoon Taste #5 Umami
  Bomb/Paste Original
  Recipe (optional)
70 g/1 scant cup Cheddar
  cheese, grated/shredded
40 g/½ cup Parmesan
  cheese, grated
nutmeg (optional)
sea salt and freshly ground
  black pepper

SERVES 4

Preheat the oven to 180°C (350°F) Gas 4.

Take a sharp knife and remove all the hard, outer leaves of the cauliflower, leaving the very fine ones from the inner layer. Cut the stalk off the bottom of the vegetable so that it sits flat. Cut an X into the bottom of the stalk – this will help the thickest part of the cauliflower cook faster so as to not overcook the florets.

Boil the cauliflower in a large pan of boiling salted water for 15–20 minutes, or until tender in the centre.

While the cauliflower is cooking, make the cheese sauce. Place the milk, flour and butter in a medium saucepan over a medium-low heat. Gradually bring to a slow simmer, whisking continuously, for about 5 minutes, or until the sauce becomes thick and smooth.

Reduce the heat to low and allow the sauce to cook very gently for 5 minutes, stirring occasionally.

Season the sauce with the Umami Bomb/Paste (if using), cheeses, nutmeg (if using), and salt and pepper.

Use a grill/broiler to grill/broil the bacon. Once cooked, chop it into squares and set aside.

Once the cauliflower is cooked, place in an ovenproof dish, pour over the cheese sauce, and dot around the tomatoes, bacon and scatter with a handful of Cheddar cheese and a grinding of black pepper. Bake in the preheated oven for about 10–15 minutes, just so that the sauce colours and begins to bubble.

Serve immediately.

Bolognese is one of those things that everyone seems to have their own secret recipe for. My recipe involves using two of my signature flavour bombs (although I've suggested alternatives too). I created these entirely for the purpose of delivering the fantastic flavours of slow-cooking fast – a real problem-solver for home-cooks in a hurry. I believe that when these flavour bombs are used together, you will be hard-pushed to find a better instant slow-cooked taste solution. That said if you cannot get hold of my products or you don't want to, you can experiment with other ingredients from your umami larder, such as soy sauce, Worcestershire sauce, an anchovy and even Marmite/yeast extract. Regarding the meat: some use all beef and some opt for a mixture of beef, pork and/or veal; duck is also a good choice because it is high in umami.

SPECIAL SPAGHETTI BOLOGNESE

2 tablespoons olive oil

150 g/5½ oz. pancetta, diced

150 g/5½ oz. Portobello or chestnut mushrooms, chopped

1 onion, very finely chopped

1 carrot, grated

1 celery stick, very finely chopped

2 garlic cloves, crushed

500 g/1 lb. 2 oz. minced/ground beef (or duck breast, very finely chopped)

1 teaspoon dried oregano

3 bay leaves

400-g/14-oz. can chopped tomatoes

2 large glasses of red wine (for extra deliciousness, you can also add an extra half glass of marsala or brandy)

4 tablespoons Taste #5 Umami Bomba! XXX tomato purée/paste, or tomato purée/paste

3 teaspoons Taste #5 Umami Bomb/Paste Original Recipe or a good splash of soy or Worcestershire sauce

sea salt and freshly ground black pepper, to taste

extra virgin olive oil

TO SERVE

spaghetti

Parmesan cheese, grated

handful flat-leaf parsley, finely chopped

SERVES 4–6

Heat the oil in a large saucepan and fry the pancetta and mushrooms for 3–4 minutes, until browned and the fat of the pancetta is rendered.

Add the onion, carrot, celery and garlic and sauté on a low heat, stirring regularly until the vegetables have begun to give off their liquid, soften and caramelize slightly. Be patient with this stage, as waiting for the vegetables to cook down and caramelize properly will add a beautiful depth of flavour to the meat.

Add the minced/ground beef to the pan and cook, stirring regularly, until browned. Add the oregano, bay leaves, tomatoes, red wine, marsala or brandy (if using), Umami Bomba XXX! tomato purée/paste (or tomato purée/paste) and Umami Bomb/Paste (or soy or Worcestershire sauce). Bring to the boil and then lower the heat, cover and simmer on a really low heat for 25–45 minutes (if you have time, you can let this simmer for up to 3 hours on a very low heat – basically the longer the better).

Taste and adjust the seasoning (this won't need much salt), and drizzle in some olive oil to finish.

Serve with al dente spaghetti, grated Parmesan cheese and chopped parsley, tossing the Bolognese all the way through the pasta.

MAPLE & BACON PANCAKES

What's not to like about the combination of pancakes, bacon and maple syrup?

125 g/1 cup plain/
   all-purpose flour,
   (spooned and levelled)
2 teaspoons caster/
   granulated sugar
1½ teaspoons baking
   powder
½ teaspoon bicarbonate
   of/baking soda
½ teaspoon salt
310 ml/1¼ cups buttermilk
2 tablespoons unsalted
   butter, melted
1 UK large, US extra large
   egg
10 rashers/slices
   streaky/fatty bacon
pure maple syrup, to serve
   (optional)

MAKES 10

Preheat the oven to 200°C (400°F) Gas 6. In a bowl, whisk together the flour, sugar, baking powder, bicarbonate of/baking soda and salt. In another bowl, whisk together the buttermilk, butter and egg. Mix the flour mixture into the buttermilk mixture until just combined, with small to medium lumps remaining.

In a large non-stick frying pan/skillet, fry the bacon until golden on both sides and just turning crisp. Drain the bacon on paper towels and set aside.

Make each bacon pancake by dropping a tablespoon of batter into the pan/skillet, top with a bacon rasher/slice, and cover with a further teaspoon of batter. Cook until some bubbles appear on top of the pancake and a few have burst, 1½–2 minutes. With a spatula, carefully flip the pancake and cook until golden. Repeat with all the bacon rashers/slices, cooking in batches if necessary and keeping the cooked pancakes warm in a low oven. Make more pancakes in the same way with any remaining batter, adding more oil to the pan if necessary. Serve with maple syrup if desired.

On a mellow and comforting scale from one to ten, I think this has to rank as a ten. So comforting and super mellow… another example of kitchen alchemy where everyday ingredients come together to create something so much more extraordinary than the sum of their simple parts.

BAKED WHITE FISH WITH SPINACH & CHEESE SAUCE

2 tablespoons butter
1 shallot or small onion,
**   very finely chopped**
2 tablespoons plain/
**   all-purpose flour**
250 ml/1 cup double/heavy
**   cream**
75 g/1 cup mature/sharp
**   Cheddar cheese,**
**   grated/shredded**
fresh nutmeg
sea salt and freshly ground
**   black pepper**
2 handfuls young-leaf
**   spinach**
2 x 200 g/7 oz. firm white
**   fish fillets (sustainable)**
small knob/pat of butter
Parmesan cheese

SERVES 2

Preheat the oven to 180°C (350°F) Gas 4.

Melt the butter. Add the shallot or onion and cook over a low heat for about 5 minutes. You want the shallot or onion to soften and go translucent in colour but not brown.

Stir in the flour and let this cook for a further minute.

Slowly pour in the cream, whisking all the time.

Add the cheese and a grating of nutmeg. Season with black pepper.

Spread a spoonful of the sauce over the bottom of a shallow Pyrex baking dish. Top with the spinach then put the fish on top. Season the fish and spinach generously with salt and freshly ground black pepper, top with a small knob/pat of butter then spoon over the rest of the sauce.

Top with a generous grating of Parmesan cheese and transfer the dish to the oven. Bake for 25–30 minutes in the preheated oven until the fish is cooked and the sauce is bubbling.

BETTER BUTTER CHICKEN

Regardless of whether you think you usually like Indian food or not, I urge you to try this wonderfully comforting dish.

150 g/1 stick plus
  2 tablespoons butter
1 onion, finely chopped
  or grated
2 garlic cloves, crushed
425 g/15 oz. passata/
  strained tomatoes
4 tablespoons Taste #5
  Umami Bomba! XXX
  tomato purée/paste
  or 3 tablespoons double
  concentrated tomato
  purée/paste
400 ml/1½ cups plus
  2 tablespoons double/
  heavy cream or one 400
  ml/14 oz. can coconut
  milk (I use half of each)

½ teaspoon cayenne pepper
1 teaspoon garam masala
5 cardamom pods, bruised
  with the back of a knife
8 curry leaves (optional)
1 teaspoon sea salt
4 large chicken breasts,
  cut into large chunks
1 tablespoon vegetable oil
2 tablespoons tandoori
  paste or 2 teaspoons
  tandoori masala powder

TO SERVE
cooked basmati rice
chopped coriander/cilantro

SERVES 4–6

Preheat the oven to 190°C (375°F) Gas 5.

Melt half the butter in a medium saucepan over a low-medium heat and fry the onion and garlic for 4–5 minutes, stirring constantly, until softened. They should not brown. Melt the remaining butter in the same saucepan and add the passata/strained tomatoes, Umami Bomba! XXX tomato purée/paste (or tomato purée/paste), cream or coconut milk (or mixture of both), cayenne pepper, garam masala, cardamom pods, curry leaves (if using) and salt. Bring to the boil, then reduce heat to low and simmer, stirring occasionally, for 15–20 minutes, or until it begins to thicken.

Meanwhile, toss the chicken pieces with the vegetable oil and tandoori paste or powder. Spread out onto a baking tray and cook in the preheated oven for 12 minutes, or until no longer pink in the centre. Once done, add the chicken and any cooking juices to the sauce and simmer for 5 minutes before serving with rice and chopped coriander/cilantro.

SHAZZA'S 'JAPANESE MUM'S' CHICKEN

This recipe is something of an urban myth. It was pointed out to me by my friend Shazza, who thought I might be interested in the Italian and Japanese mix. I have tweaked the recipe from the original because I found the vinegar a little overpowering (sorry Tomoko's mum), but I hope you will like it. So far, it has had 936 likes online so it can't be bad. Aside from being packed with umami this is a very easy and quick and popular one-pot dish.

8 chicken drumsticks,
  skin on
250 ml/1 cup water
6 tablespoons balsamic
  vinegar
6 tablespoons soy sauce
6 tablespoons honey
6 tablespoons tomato
  ketchup

1 tablespoon Taste #5
  Umami Bomb/Paste
  Original Recipe
3 garlic cloves, peeled
  and bruised
2 red chillies/chiles, split
  open, seeds removed

SERVES 4–6

Place all the ingredients in a saucepan over a high heat.

Bring to the boil, then turn down the heat a little to a strong simmer. Cook for about 20 minutes, removing any scum that rises to the surface.

Be sure to turn and baste the drumsticks frequently in the liquid. At the end of the cooking time, you want the liquid to have reduced to a sticky glaze. If you feel that the chicken is over-cooking, carefully remove it from the pan and add it back once the glaze has reduced.

Arrange the chicken on a serving platter, and spoon over the glaze.

Blue cheese and salad have been served together for a long, long time; the iceberg wedge and blue cheese dressing is a very popular appetizer in restaurants all over the world, for example. This recipe works on that same principle that salad and blue cheese go together well, especially with a sweet element like grapes or pear. Roquefort is very high in umami, as are walnuts. Hold on to your seat and let this super-quick but rather chic salad transport you to a place of fruity, savoury deliciousness.

ENDIVE & ROQUEFORT SALAD WITH GRAPES & CARAMELIZED WALNUTS

3 red chicory/endives (yellow if you can't find red)

250 g/1⅔ cups white grapes, halved (red if using yellow endive)

20 radishes, thinly sliced

150 g/1 cup plus 1 tablespoon Roquefort, cut into cubes the size of a postage stamp

4 handfuls of watercress (any mixed green leaves will do, though)

CARAMELIZED WALNUTS

75 g/scant ½ cup walnut halves, snapped in half

3 tablespoons brown sugar

½ teaspoon salt

pinch cayenne

1½ teaspoons walnut oil

DRESSING

6 tablespoons extra virgin olive oil

2 tablespoons white wine vinegar

2 teaspoons Dijon mustard

sea salt and freshly ground black pepper, to taste

1 bunch chives, snipped

freshly squeezed lemon juice

runny honey (optional)

SERVES 4–6

Caramelize the walnuts by putting them in a frying pan/skillet over a medium-high heat with the sugar, salt, cayenne and walnut oil. Cook until the sugar is caramelized, stirring occasionally to make sure all the nuts are coated.

Discard the outer leaves of the chicory/endives, then separate and cut the inner leaves in half lengthways and cut into rings.

In a large salad bowl, combine all of the salad ingredients.

Make the dressing by whisking the oil, vinegar and mustard together really well until emulsified. Season and add the chives and a good squeeze of lemon juice, to taste and a drop of honey, if using.

Drizzle the dressing over the salad so that all the ingredients are well coated.

Serve immediately.

The 'mantecatura' (the finishing stage, done off the heat) is the key to this recipe, as well as continuously stirring the pot. Risotto is one of those things where you get out what you put into it; the more energy you give it the creamier it will taste….To make it more indulgent, top it with a dollop of mascarpone and a grinding of black pepper to serve. You can also ring the changes by replacing the lemon zest with orange zest – the possibilities are truly endless. For other risottos high in umami, you can replace the asparagus with mushrooms, garden peas and sweet potato, or make a *Primavera*, which is a mix of diced carrot, courgette/zucchini, potato, peas, and asparagus tips.

ASPARAGUS, LEMON & BASIL RISOTTO

475 g/1 lb. fresh green asparagus

1 onion, very finely chopped in a food processor (the same size as the grains of rice)

40 g/3 tablespoons butter or olive oil

320 g/1¾ cups Arborio rice (1 fistful per person plus 2 for the pot)

125 ml/1 small glass dry white wine

1 litre/quart hot chicken or vegetable stock, or 2 stock cubes dissolved in 1 litre/quart of boiling water

sea salt and freshly ground black pepper

grated zest of 1 unwaxed lemon

handful of torn basil leaves

MANTECATURA (TO FINISH)

60 g/4 tablespoons cold butter, cut into small cubes

85 g/1¼ cups finely grated Parmesan cheese

SERVES 4

Prepare the 60 g/4 tablespoons butter and the cheese for the *mantecatura* and keep in the fridge until needed at the end.

Cut off the asparagus tips and set them aside. Chop the remaining stalks into fingernail-sized pieces, discarding the woody ends.

In a large heavy-based saucepan, sauté the onion in the butter or olive oil until soft. Add the stalks of the asparagus and cook for 1–2 minutes.

Add the rice and stir until translucent and glassy. Do not allow the butter to overheat or any of the ingredients to brown. Add the wine and stir well until evaporated.

Add a ladleful of hot stock and simmer, stirring all the time with a wooden spoon. As the stock is absorbed, continue to add a ladleful at a time, still stirring. Remember, the more you stir, the creamier the risotto! When all the stock has been incorporated, your rice should be soft on the outside with a firm centre and the risotto should be nice and creamy. This will take about 18 minutes. With the last ladle of stock, add the asparagus tips – this is to ensure that they stay crisp and green.

Remove the pan from the heat and beat in the butter and Parmesan cheese (the mantecatura). Add the lemon zest and basil and adjust the seasoning. Serve immediately.

NOTE: For a looser risotto with less bite, add a little extra stock on a high heat so as not to overcook the rice.

This is an extra special mac 'n' cheese, the kind you are served in a restaurant as a side or good enough to serve at a dinner party. It differs from a traditional M&C in that it is cream-based and not white-sauce based. This means that it does not dry up the way that baked white sauce ones can, because you are literally tossing the hot macaroni in the sauce, keeping things very loose and then serving it. However, if you are a traditionalist or looking for a quick midweek dinner using the more familiar white sauce method, please check out the Umami Mac 'n' Cheese on my website: laurasanttini.com.

TRUFFLED MAC 'N' CHEESE

950 ml/4 cups
   double/heavy cream
¼ teaspoon freshly
   grated nutmeg
¼ teaspoon cayenne
   pepper
I bay leaf
2 tablespoons butter
4 shallots, finely
   chopped
3 garlic cloves, crushed
I salted anchovy fillet
500 ml/2 cups dry white
   wine
100 g/1 cup plus
   2 tablespoons
   Cheddar cheese,
   grated/shredded
100 g/1 cup plus
   2 tablespoons
   Gruyère cheese,
   grated/shredded

45 g/⅔ cup Parmesan
   cheese, grated
2 tablespoons black
   truffle oil
sea salt and freshly
   ground black pepper
500 g/1 lb. 2 oz.
   macaroni pasta

TO SERVE
75 g/scant 2 cups
   toasted Panko
   breadcrumbs
I tablespoon flat-leaf
   parsley, finely chopped
25 g/⅓ cup Parmesan
   cheese

SERVES 8

In a large heavy-based saucepan, heat the cream until it almost boiling, then turn down the heat, add the nutmeg, cayenne pepper and bay leaf and allow to simmer slowly until reduced by half. Set aside.

In a medium saucepan, heat the butter until melted then sauté the shallots, garlic and anchovy until the anchovy has melted and the shallots are soft and translucent but not browned.

Pour in the wine and simmer until most of the wine has evaporated.

Pour the cream mixture into the shallot and wine mixture. Add the cheeses, truffle oil and season to taste. Set aside.

Meanwhile, fill a large saucepan with salted water and bring to the boil. Add the pasta and cook until al dente. Transfer the macaroni to a colander and drain, reserving a small amount of the pasta cooking water.

Return the pasta to its cooking pot and add just enough truffled sauce to coat the pasta (you want it nice and creamy but not too rich), along with 3–4 tablespoons of the pasta cooking water. Return to the heat for I minute, and give everything a good mix to make it extra creamy. Pour into a suitable serving dish.

To serve, mix the breadcrumbs, the parsley and the Parmesan cheese together and sprinkle over the dish. Serve immediately.

NOTE: This recipe makes more sauce than you will need for the 500 g/1 lb. 2 oz. pasta, but you can keep the rest in the fridge or freeze it for future use.

The principle of rolling something in grated Parmesan cheese and wrapping it in prosciutto is a perfect way to create umami synergy and can be applied to anything from asparagus or a scallop to a chicken breast or a fish fillet. If using ingredients like fish and meat, just season and drizzle with a little olive oil and bake (remembering to baste throughout cooking with a splash of wine or stock). This recipe can be served as a simple appetizer or as a snack. It isn't a crime to use shop-bought tapenade, but just let it down with a little extra virgin olive oil. You can let your hair down too…

PROSCIUTTO & MOZZARELLA BITES WITH BLACK OLIVE TAPENADE

MOZZARELLA BITES
1–2 handfuls grated
    Parmesan cheese
4 basil leaves, finely
    chopped
generous grinding
    of black pepper
12 bocconcini di
    mozzarella
    (mozzarella balls)
extra virgin olive oil
12 slices prosciutto

BLACK OLIVE TAPENADE
250 g/2½ cups
    stoned/pitted black
    olives (Taggiasche or
    Kalamata)
3 tablespoons capers,
    finely chopped
4–6 anchovy fillets in oil,
    finely chopped

1 garlic clove, peeled
    and crushed
100 ml/7 tablespoons
    olive oil
handful of flat-leaf
    parsley, finely chopped
sea salt and freshly
    ground black pepper
freshly squeezed juice
    of 1 lemon

TO SERVE
4 handfuls
    chicory/endive
2 tablespoons tapenade
extra virgin olive oil

SERVES 4

To make a coarser tapenade, simply mix all ingredients together and season with salt, ground black pepper and lemon juice to taste. For a smoother paste place all the ingredients in a food processor and pulse until you reach the required consistency. Set aside.

Mix together the Parmesan cheese, basil and black pepper.

Roll each mozzarella ball in a little olive oil, then in the Parmesan mixture and finally wrap up in a slice of prosciutto.

Fry the mozzarella wraps in a little oil in a non-stick pan/skillet over a high heat for a few minutes until the prosciutto begins to colour and crisp and the mozzarella begins to melt.

Let down the tapenade with a couple of tablespoons of oil.

Serve the mozzarella balls on some chicory/endive, drizzle with the tapenade dressing and olive oil and finish with a grinding of black pepper. Serve immediately.

There is nothing more mellow and comforting than a bowl of creamy, umami-packed pasta, served with a glass of chilled white wine. It makes having a bad day almost worthwhile… Cacio e Pepe ('cheese and pepper') is a famous dish from Rome, traditionally made with lots of black pepper and Pecorino cheese. Another Roman creation, Alfredo's rich sauce is dolce vita living at its most indulgent. Carbonara's (see photo, right) dreamy, creamy combination of Parmesan and pancetta is a worldwide favourite. All three of these recipes serve 4 and make enough to coat 400 g/14 oz. spaghetti.

CACIO E PEPE

8 tablespoons extra virgin olive oil

4 teaspoons freshly ground black pepper

200 g/2⅔ cups grated Pecorino Romano/ Parmesan or a mix of both

Cook the spaghetti and drain, but reserve some of the cooking water.

Put the oil and the pepper in a frying pan/skillet, along with 4 tablespoons of reserved hot pasta water.

Add the spaghetti and sauté for a few moments until most of the pasta water has evaporated. Add most of the cheese and give one final toss to combine. Divide the spaghetti between bowls and finish with more cheese and another generous grinding of black pepper.

ALFREDO

400 ml/1⅔ cups double/heavy cream

250 g/2 sticks plus 2 tablespoons very fresh unsalted butter

150 g/2 cups grated Parmesan cheese or

75 g/1 cup Parmesan cheese and 75 g/1 cup Pecorino cheese

pinch of freshly grated nutmeg

salt flakes and white pepper

Heat 300 ml/1¼ cups of the cream and all the butter in a heavy-based saucepan over a medium heat for about 2–3 minutes, stirring occasionally, until the butter has melted into the cream. Stir in the cheese and remove from the heat.

Add the drained cooked spaghetti and toss with the remaining cream and nutmeg. (If the sauce is too runny, heat over a low heat until it is thickened).

Season carefully – this dish rarely needs salt – and serve.

CARBONARA

3 tablespoons olive oil

150 g/5½ oz. pancetta or bacon, cut into strips

4 fresh egg yolks (use only very fresh eggs)

splash of double/heavy cream (optional)

4 tablespoons grated Parmesan cheese

freshly ground black pepper

1 tablespoons chopped flat-leaf parsley

Heat the olive oil in a large frying pan/skillet. Add the pancetta or bacon and fry until it is browned but not too crisp. Set aside.

Place the egg yolks, cream (if using) and cheese in a large serving bowl and a generous grinding of black pepper. Mix well with a fork.

Drain your pasta and add immediately to the cheese and egg mixture. Add the pancetta or bacon and parsley, and toss well until all is well mixed and creamy.

This ubiquitous cheeseburger is probably the most popular way to experience umami in the Western world, and that's why we're lovin' it. The meat, combined with the cheese and ketchup, is really not that different to the meat, tomato and Parmesan in a Bolognese. Total umami synergy and again no doubt why they are amongst the world's most popular dishes. This recipe was featured in my book *Flash Cooking* under the heading 'All Burger No Bum' as it is a bun-free burger. The quantity of meat will make 4 regular-sized burgers, or 2 if you're feeling really hungry. If you cannot live without the bun, I would suggest using a tasty brioche-style bun, because its sweetness will maximize the umami even further. The question is now you have built it, can you get your mouth around it?!

MY FAVOURITE BURGER

1 medium red onion
500 g/1 lb. 2 oz. lean minced/ground beef
1 egg yolk
squeeze of Taste #5 Umami Bomb/Paste Original Recipe or tomato purée/paste (optional)
dash of Worcestershire sauce
handful of flat-leaf parsley, finely chopped
sea salt and freshly ground black pepper

MARIE ROSE SAUCE
2 tablespoons mayonnaise
1 tablespoon tomato ketchup
1 teaspoon Worcestershire sauce
1 teaspoon Cognac or brandy

dash of Tabasco Sauce
freshly squeezed lemon juice to taste
pinch of paprika
pinch of salt

TO SERVE
4 Portobello mushrooms
8 thin slices of Parmesan cheese or mature hard Pecorino cheese
12 rashers/slices smoked maple-cured streaky/fatty bacon, cooked until crisp
8 crisp lettuce leaves
1 large beef tomato, sliced
2 large sweet pickles, sliced lengthways

**MAKES 4
(OR 2 IF YOU'RE
VERY HUNGRY)**

Halve the onion and cut a thick slice from each half, then separate these into rings and set aside. Finely chop the remaining onion.

In a large bowl, mix together the chopped onion with the minced/ground beef, egg yolk, Umami Bomb/Paste or tomato purée/paste (if using), Worcestershire sauce and parsley. Season well and divide the mixture into 4 (or 2) chunky burgers. Cover with clingfilm/plastic wrap and chill for 25–30 minutes.

When ready to cook, preheat the oven to 180°C (350°F) Gas 4 and make the Marie Rose Sauce by mixing together all the ingredients.

Place the chilled burgers on a lightly oiled tray and cook in the preheated oven for 25 minutes.

Place the mushrooms on a baking tray, season and drizzle with a little olive oil. Cook in the preheated oven until just softened (but not too much as this will be your 'bun').

To serve, stack in the following order from the bottom up: mushroom, lettuce, tomato, reserved rings of onion, burger, sauce, cheese, pickle, bacon.

I usually call this 'Quick Cottage Pie', because I make it without the usual, carrot and celery soffrito. This is a take on my grandmother's ragout, which she made by cutting an onion into quarters and frying it in a little olive oil with 2 cloves of crushed garlic. Once the onions were translucent, she added the minced/ground beef and cooked it until browned. Then she would add a good squeeze of tomato purée/paste, bay leaves and a whole glass of wine and leave to simmer. This ragout is wonderful on pasta and equally, with the onions chopped more finely, it makes the perfect no-hassle base for a tasty midweek cottage pie.

SWEET POTATO COTTAGE PIE

I tablespoon olive oil
I onion, finely chopped
I garlic clove, crushed
500 g/I lb. 2 oz.
   minced/ground beef
2 tablespoons double
   concentrated tomato
   purée/tomato paste or
   Taste #5 Umami Bomba!
   XXX tomato purée/paste
small pinch ground
   cinnamon
small pinch grated nutmeg
2 bay leaves
125 ml/½ cup glass red wine
250 g/9 oz. potatoes
750 g/I lb. 10½ oz. sweet
   potatoes
30 g/2 tablespoons butter
125 ml/½ cup milk, warmed
grated nutmeg (optional)
I handful finely grated
   Parmesan cheese
sea salt and freshly ground
   black pepper

SERVES 4

Preheat the oven to 175°C (350°F) Gas 4.

Heat the olive oil in a large, heavy-based saucepan and fry the onion over a medium heat for 4–5 minutes, until soft and translucent. Add the garlic and fry for a further minute.

Add the minced/ground beef and fry for about 5 minutes, or until well browned. Add the tomato purée/paste or Umami Bomba! XXX tomato purée/paste, cinnamon, nutmeg, bay leaves and wine, and simmer over a low heat for 10–15 minutes.

Meanwhile, peel the potatoes and sweet potatoes, cutting them into 4-cm/1½-in. cubes. Cook them in salted boiling water for about 10–12 minutes, or until tender. Drain the potatoes and return to the pan. Add the butter, then while beginning to mash, gradually add the warm milk (you may not need all of it), the nutmeg (if using) and the Parmesan cheese. Season to taste.

Pour the minced/ground beef mixture into an ovenproof dish and cover with the mashed potato. Cook in the oven for 30–40 minutes until golden brown and bubbling. Leave to stand for 5 minutes before serving.

I have loved Heinz tomato soup forever. When I was a child, a bowl of this almost too sweet soup would appear when I was in bed, ill. My family never ate anything out of a can because both my parents always cooked from scratch, but contrary to any logic, when I was unwell and had no appetite this warm bowl of orange soup was all it took to lift my little spirits. This recipe is the closest thing you will ever come to Heinz tomato soup at home. I'm not sure if that is a good or bad thing, but either way it is delicious and super comforting to me.

COMFORTING TOMATO SOUP

90 g/6 tablespoons butter
1 medium white onion, diced
2 x 400-g/14-oz. cans chopped tomatoes
1.5 litres/quarts tomato juice
2 tablespoons sugar or runny honey (or to taste and depending on how acidic your tomatoes are)
2 chicken stock cubes
freshly ground black pepper
1 handful flat-leaf parsley, chopped
1 handful fresh basil, chopped

SERVES 4–6

Melt all the butter in a large pot over a medium heat. Once melted, add the onion and cook until translucent.

Add the chopped tomatoes, tomato juice and sugar or honey. Stir to combine.

Add the chicken stock cubes and some freshly ground black pepper and stir well. Allow the soup to boil for 20–30 minutes.

Turn off the heat and using a stick blender, blend the soup until it is completely smooth.

Stir in the fresh herbs and serve.

An adaptation of an Italian classic, this is a wonderfully robust yet, remarkably clean soup.

HEARTY ITALIAN SOUP

1 tablespoon olive oil
75 g/2½ oz. pancetta, finely chopped
1 onion, finely chopped
1 carrots, chopped
3 garlic cloves, chopped
3 bay leaves
200 g/3 cups fresh shiitake mushrooms
200 g/3 cups chestnut mushrooms
a small handful of dried porcini mushrooms, soaked in 250 ml/1 cup hot water
200 g/1 cup puy/French green lentils
1 tablespoon tomato purée/paste
1 large glass (175 ml/¾ cup) red wine
2 tablespoons soy sauce
1 can chopped tomatoes plus 1 can of water
2 chicken stock cubes with 1 litre/quart of water
100 g/3½ oz. cavolo nero, chopped or baby spinach
chopped flat-leaf parsley, to serve
grated Pecorino cheese, to serve
extra virgin olive oil, to serve

SERVES 4–6

Heat the oil in a large, heavy-based saucepan, brown the pancetta, remove and set aside. Add the onion, celery, carrots, garlic and bay leaves, then continue to cook over a low heat until the onion is soft and glassy but not coloured. Add the fresh mushrooms and stir well until they have absorbed all the soffrito juices and begin to soften.

Do not drain the porcini mushrooms, but remove them from the hot water with a slotted spoon and finely chop, reserving the soaking juice. Add the porcini mushrooms and lentils and stir well. Cook for 2–3 minutes, then add the cooked pancetta, tomato purée/paste, red wine and soy sauce.

Turn up the heat and, once the red wine has almost evaporated, pour in the reserved porcini mushroom liquid, taking care not to let any of the gritty bits fall into the pot. Add the stock. Reduce the heat and simmer for about 30 minutes, or until the lentils are cooked but not too soft.

Give the soup a good stir then ladle it into deep bowls and scatter the parsley, Pecorino cheese and a drizzle of olive oil.

This is my favourite salmon dish and we usually have it at least once a week at home. Take care not to overdo the maple syrup (very tempting, I know) as the dish loses something if it is too sweet. This method also works very well with chicken thighs and for roasting vegetables.

MAPLE SOY SALMON

60 ml/¼ cup maple syrup
1 tablespoon soy sauce
1–2 garlic cloves, crushed
pinch of ground ginger or
    a 2.5-cm/1-in. piece of
    grated fresh ginger
1 teaspoon Taste #5 Umami
    Bomb/Paste (Vegetarian
    Garlic)
sea salt and freshly ground
    black pepper
2 salmon fillets

SERVES 2

In a small bowl, mix together the maple syrup, soy sauce, garlic, ginger and Umami Bomb/ Paste and season to taste with salt and pepper.

Place the salmon fillets in an ovenproof dish and coat them on all sides with the mixture. If time permits, cover with clingfilm/plastic wrap and leave to marinate in the refrigerator for 30–60 minutes.

When ready to cook, preheat the oven to 200°C (400°F) Gas 6.

Cook the salmon in the ovenproof dish, uncovered, for around 15–30 minutes, until its centre is cooked through.

This is probably one of the most popular dishes from my first book *Easy Tasty Italian* and one people tell me they cook all the time. I wonder if it is because it is delicious and quickly prepped in one pot or if it is because with a cooking time of 6 hours, you have plenty of time to do all sorts of things, like drink coffee and read the Sunday newspapers!?

LEG-OVER LAMB

2 kg/4½ lbs. leg of lamb

4 garlic cloves, each cut into 3 pieces

3 salted anchovies, each cut into 4 pieces

2 rosemary sprigs, cut into 2.5-cm/1-in. lengths

3 tablespoons olive oil

sea salt and freshly ground black pepper

4 red onions, cut into quarters

350 ml/1¼ cups plus 3 tablespoons red wine

125 ml/½ cup port (if you do not have any, increase the amount of wine to 475 ml/ 2 cups minus 2 tablespoons)

1–2 tablespoons herb or berry jam/jelly (such as mint, rosemary, redcurrant or sage)

1 tablespoon balsamic vinegar (the thick type)

1 tablespoon chopped fresh rosemary

1 tablespoon chopped fresh sage

1 tablespoon chopped fresh mint

bite-sized roast potatoes, to serve

SERVES 4–6

Preheat the oven to 120°C (250°F) Gas ½.

Make random slits in the lamb with a sharp knife, and stuff each hole with a piece of garlic, a piece of anchovy and some rosemary, using your finger or the end of a wooden spoon to poke them right in.

Heat the olive oil in a large casserole dish, add the lamb and brown it well on all sides. Season with salt and pepper, and add the onions, red wine and port.

Mix the herb or berry jam/jelly, balsamic vinegar and fresh herbs together, and spoon over the lamb. Cover with a tight-fitting lid and cook in the oven for around 5–6 hours, until the meat is falling off the bone.

Serve with crispy bite-sized roast potatoes, garnished with lemon slices and rosemary.

My grandmother used to make me peas with pancetta as a side dish. She used sludgy-green petit pois from a tin, but it also works with frozen petit pois. In my mind tiny tinned peas make this recipe infinitely more delicious, though! Ham and peas are a classic combination and this simple dish is a perfect illustration of 'umami synergy' where the sweetness of the onions and peas combine with the salty pancetta to prove that magic umami formula $1+1 = 8$, that is to say that when skilfully combined, umami-containing ingredients can boost each other to give you six extra flavour points. Eggs also contain umami, so the flavour maths on this is undeniable.

PEAS, HAM & EGGS

1 glug olive oil
100 g/3½ oz. cubed
   pancetta or bacon,
   chopped into strips
1 onion, thinly sliced
1 garlic cloves, thinly sliced
425 g/15 oz. frozen or
   tinned petit pois peas
100 ml/7 tablespoons
   chicken stock
1 sprig of mint, leaves only
4 UK large, US extra large
   eggs at room
   temperature
1 fresh mint sprig, leaves
   only, chopped
sea salt and freshly ground
   black pepper

SERVES 4

Heat a glug of olive oil in a large frying pan/skillet and sauté the pancetta or bacon.

When cooked through, add the onion slices and garlic.

Sauté until the onion begins to colour and the pancetta or bacon begins to crisp up.

Add the peas to the pan with the stock and the mint, season with a little black pepper and leave to cook on a low heat with the lid on until most of the stock has evaporated. Adjust the seasoning if necessary and set aside.

Fill a medium saucepan with water and bring to the boil. Once boiling, add the eggs and time for 6–7 minutes, as you want them gooey in the middle. Remove the eggs with a slotted spoon and refresh in cold water to stop them from cooking any more.

Peel the eggs and slice them in half lengthways.

Season the eggs with a sprinkling of sea salt and black pepper and place on top of the warm peas. Serve immediately.

BOLD & BRIGHT

This recipe is well worth trying – it will not disappoint you and if you love it as much as I do, it will become one of your one-tray favourites. I usually get this ready (except for the potatoes, lemon juice and Pecorino cheese) on a Saturday and leave in the fridge overnight, so the next day all I have to do is peel a few potatoes, mix through the lemon juice and zest, sprinkle with Pecorino and throw the whole lot in the oven. When cooked the meat should be finger-licking sticky and the potatoes nicely coloured.

PECORINO LAMB

800 g/1¾ lbs. lamb
   shoulder on the bone,
   cut into large 8-cm/
   3-in. pieces
3–4 large roasting
   potatoes, cut into
   chunks for roasting
400 g/2½ cups ripe
   tomatoes, deseeded
   and chopped
1 tablespoon fennel
   seeds
2 red onions, sliced
1 celery stalk, sliced
3 garlic cloves, thinly
   sliced
handful of chopped
   flat-leaf parsley
sprig of rosemary
   (leaves only)

handful of chopped
   fresh oregano
150 ml/½ cup plus
   1 tablespoon olive oil
freshly squeezed juice
   and a piece of zest
   from 2 lemons
60 g/¾ cup Pecorino
   cheese, finely grated
splash of white wine and
   stock, for basting
   (optional)
handful of chopped
   fresh mint, to serve

SERVES 4

Preheat the oven to 180°C (350°F) Gas 4.

Place all the ingredients, except the oil, lemons, cheese and mint, flat in a large roasting tray. Generously douse in olive oil and lemon juice and zest, season with salt and pepper, and mix together well with your hands. Sprinkle with the Pecorino cheese and splash with more olive oil.

Bake in the oven for about 1 hour 20 minutes. During cooking, you can baste with a splash of white wine and/or a splash of stock, if you like. If the meat looks as if it is burning at any time, cover it with foil.

Serve sprinkled with the mint.

Everyone so far who has tried it, loves this recipe, so I call it 'happy dahl' as it always makes me feel like I am doing something right! For ease, you could use a tablespoon of curry powder instead of the spices listed below. You want the consistency to be slightly runny, so you may need to add a little water if it looks too dry. Serve with rice, tangy turmeric yogurt and plenty of fresh coriander/cilantro.

BROCCOLI & CHERRY TOMATO DAHL

65 g/4 tablespoons butter

1 large onion, halved then sliced

2 teaspoons ground cumin

1 teaspoon ground coriander

¼ teaspoon cayenne pepper

2 teaspoons turmeric

3 cardamom pods

½ teaspoon ground black pepper

200 g/1 cup plus 2 tablespoons red lentils

750 ml/3 cups chicken stock

freshly squeezed juice of 1 lemon

40 g/½ cup desiccated/dried, shredded coconut

sea salt

1 medium head of broccoli, cut into small florets

200 g/7 oz. cherry tomatoes (approx. 16–18), halved

handful fresh coriander/cilantro, finely chopped

TURMERIC YOGURT

3 tablespoons Greek-style yogurt

1 teaspoon ground turmeric

1 tablespoon chopped coriander/cilantro

1 teaspoon of mango and/or lime chutney

SERVES 4

Heat the butter in a heavy-based saucepan, and sauté the onion until golden.

Add the cumin, ground coriander, cayenne pepper, turmeric, cardamom pods and black pepper and fry for 1 minute.

Add the lentils and stir, making sure they are coated in all the spices.

Add the stock, lemon juice and the coconut. Season with salt.

Once boiling, reduce the heat and simmer for 40–45 minutes until the lentils are cooked. If the liquid evaporates too quickly, you can add some more from the kettle. The mixture should not be dry – it should be a soft, slightly sloppy, dahl consistency.

Meanwhile, make the turmeric yogurt by combining all the ingredients in a small bowl and mixing well.

Five minutes before the lentils are done, add the broccoli florets. Stir gently. Cover with a lid and simmer for 5 minutes.

Add the cherry tomatoes cover for another 3–4 minutes.

Test the broccoli – you want it to still have a bite, as it will continue to cook off the heat. If you let it overcook now, it will go mushy by the time you serve.

Divide between bowls, top with chopped coriander/cilantro and serve with the turmeric yogurt.

This is a deliciously vibrant salad that can be served either as a light meal or as a quick and easy-to-prepare appetizer. The chilli and chorizo give the dish a tasty heat, which brings out the sweetness of the calamari.

These melt-in-the-mouth umami pods are my worst enemy on holidays in Spain, because I can literally eat a whole plateful before I have even ordered my meal. I like to serve these with a paprika-seasoned aioli — well, you might as well!

CALAMARI & CHORIZO SALAD

1 tablespoon olive oil
2 garlic cloves, thinly sliced
1 fresh red chilli/chile, finely chopped and deseeded if you wish
200 g/7 oz. calamari (squid), cleaned; bodies cut into ½-cm/¼-in. thick rings
1 tablespoon tomato purée/paste or Taste #5 Umami Bomba! XXX tomato purée/paste
½ x 400-g/14-oz. can chickpeas, drained
5-cm/2-in. chunk of chorizo sausage, chopped

1 tablespoon freshly squeezed lemon juice
3 teaspoons grated lemon zest
1 teaspoon runny honey (not needed if using Umami Bomba! XXX purée/paste)
splash of white wine
1 handful of flat-leaf parsley, finely chopped
2 handfuls rocket/arugula leaves
crusty bread, to serve

SERVES 2

Heat the oil in a large frying pan/skillet over a medium heat. Add the garlic and chilli/chile and fry for 1 minute. Add the calamari, tomato purée/paste (or Umami Bomba! XXX tomato purée/paste), chickpeas and chorizo and give it all a good stir. Fry until the calamari is just cooked, about 2–3 minutes.

Add the lemon juice, zest, honey (unless you've used Umami Bomba! XXX earlier on) and the white wine and let all this bubble away for a further minute.

Toss the calamari mixture with the parsley and rocket/arugula and serve with some crusty bread.

JAMON & MANCHEGO CROQUETAS

45 g/3 tablespoons butter
70 g/½ cup tablespoons plain/all-purpose flour, plus more for rolling
450 ml/2¾ cups whole milk
100 g/3½ oz. (approximately 6 slices) finely chopped Serrano ham or Prosciutto di Parma

60 g/1 cup Manchego or Parmesan cheese, finely grated/shredded
coarse salt and freshly ground pepper
freshly grated nutmeg
2 UK large, US extra large eggs
100 g/1¾ cups fresh breadcrumbs
vegetable oil, for frying

MAKES ABOUT 15

Place the butter in a medium saucepan over a medium heat and melt. Add the flour and cook, stirring, for a couple of minutes. Add the milk slowly, whisking continuously. Let the mixture come to a low boil, while whisking, in order to cook out the flour and thicken the sauce. Once thick, whisk in the ham and cheese. Season with salt and pepper as desired and a grating of nutmeg.

Spread the mixture onto a baking sheet, and let it cool completely. Cover the surface with clingfilm/plastic wrap so it does not discolour. If you're not using it immediately, this mixture can be kept in the fridge for a couple of days.

When ready to fry, beat the eggs in a bowl and put the breadcrumbs on a plate. Cut the cooled mixture into squares (with each equating to roughly a tablespoonful), flour your hands and roll the squares into 4-cm/1½-in. ovals. One at a time, dip each oval in the egg, then roll it in the breadcrumbs. Transfer to a non-stick tray until ready to fry.

Make sure that the croquetas are at room temperature before deep-frying in batches until deep golden. Place on paper towels to drain any excess oil and serve immediately.

I love this melt-in-the-mouth classic — it is super easy to make and the result is always high-impact. I have umamified my favourite Rendang recipe which is by Donna Hay, by adding tomato purée/paste and tamarind. Rendang is where flavour meets functionality, since it was originally an Indonesian cooking method used to preserve meat before refrigeration. The pungent paste is packed with antibacterial aromatics such as garlic, tamarind and galangal, which once rubbed in to the meat are slow cooked to form a dark tasty outer coating. Historically, this would help to keep the meat from spoiling in the hot weather.

BEEF RENDANG

1 tablespoon vegetable oil
1.5 kg/3¼ lbs. beef brisket, halved
sea salt flakes
a batch of rendang curry paste (see below)
7 kaffir lime leaves
1 lemongrass stalk, bruised
1 cinnamon stick
2 x 440-ml/14-oz. cans coconut milk plus 1 can water
2 tablespoons fish sauce
freshly squeezed juice of 4 limes (approx. 60 ml/4 tablespoons)

RENDANG CURRY PASTE
2 tablespoons coriander seeds
¼ teaspoon white peppercorns
40 g/½ cup desiccated/dried shredded coconut

2 French shallots, roughly chopped
4 garlic cloves, roughly chopped
1 fresh long red chilli/chile, roughly chopped (this makes it fairly hot – deseed one for less heat)
2.5 cm/1 in. piece of fresh ginger, sliced
1 lemongrass stalk, white part only, sliced
4 kaffir lime leaves, shredded
1 teaspoon dried turmeric
1 teaspoon galangal paste
1 tablespoon dark brown sugar
2 tablespoons sesame oil
½ tablespoon tomato purée/paste
1 teaspoon tamarind paste (optional)

SERVES 4–6

To make the Rendang curry paste, heat a small frying pan/skillet over a medium heat. Add the coriander seeds and peppercorns and toast, shaking the pan frequently, for about 2 minutes until they become fragrant. Add the coconut to the pan and toast for another minute until the coconut becomes a lovely golden colour.

Place in a small food processor and process until ground.

Add the rest of the ingredients and process, scraping down the sides of the bowl, until smooth.

Preheat the oven to 180°C (350°F) Gas 4.

Heat the oil over a high heat in a large ovenproof pot with a tight-fitting lid. Sprinkle the beef with a little salt on both sides. Brown the beef well on both sides, about 5 minutes each side. Set aside.

Turn the heat down slightly to medium-high. Add the curry paste to the pot and cook, stirring constantly, for 1–2 minutes to release the aromatics.

Add the rest of the ingredients and bring to the boil. Place the beef in the liquid, cover the pot, and place in the preheated oven.

Cook for 2 hours, then turn the meat and continue cooking, uncovered, for another 1 hour. Turn the meat a couple of times during cooking to ensure that it is constantly basted with sauce. The sauce should be reduced and the beef lovely and tender, almost spoonable.

SIMPLE BAKED EGG

This sunny and quick, low-calorie, high-protein breakfast, dinner or appetizer is a great way to use up any leftover tomato sauce. It can also be made with a good-quality shop-bought tomato sauce. If you really want to take things to another level and forget the low-calorie benefits, you can add a dollop of mascarpone cheese before you add the eggs. Serve with strips of sourdough bread for dunking.

3 tablespoons Really Red Sauce (see page 169)
1–2 free range eggs
sea salt and freshly ground black pepper

1 heaped teaspoon finely grated Parmesan cheese
sourdough bread, in strips

SERVES 1

Preheat the oven to 180°C (350°F) Gas 4.

Simply put the tomato sauce into a large single-serve ramekin and crack in the egg(s) on top of the sauce. Season with some salt and freshly ground black pepper and sprinkle over some Parmesan cheese (about 1 teaspoon but if you want you can add more or less.)

Transfer to the preheated oven and cook for 8–10 minutes (the egg white should be cooked through but the yolk(s) still soft).

CHORIZO CORNBREAD

Some do and some don't add sugar to cornbread – apparently it is not the done thing – but then again I feel that a teaspoon of sugar really amplifies the umami pop in this ridiculously tempting side dish.

150 g/5½ oz. chorizo, finely diced
540 g/3¾ cups polenta/cornmeal
4 teaspoons bicarbonate of/baking soda
2 teaspoons salt
1–2 tablespoons sugar (optional)

750 ml/3 cups buttermilk
2 eggs
2 tablespoons tomato purée/paste
170 g/1½ sticks unsalted butter, melted
olive oil

SERVES 8

Preheat the oven to 200°C (400°F) Gas 6.

Place a 30-cm/12-in. (ovenproof) cast-iron frying pan/skillet onto a medium heat. Once hot, add the chorizo and fry until the red oils escape and the chorizo is browned around the edges. Remove the chorizo and set aside but leave the remaining oil in the pan/skillet as you will need it later.

Mix together the polenta/cornmeal, bicarbonate of/baking soda, salt and sugar (if using) in a large bowl.

In another bowl, combine the buttermilk, eggs, tomato purée/paste and melted butter.

Pour the wet ingredients onto the dry ingredients and give everything a good stir to combine. Add the chorizo pieces back in and stir again.

Put the pan/skillet back over a medium heat. You need about 2 tablespoons of oil at the bottom of the pan/skillet. If the chorizo didn't give off enough oil, add some olive oil. Once the oil is hot, pour in the batter and spread evenly with a spatula.

Transfer to the preheated oven and bake for 25–30 minutes until the top is golden brown and a skewer comes out clean when inserted into the middle.

Leave to rest for 10–20 minutes before serving.

Another recipe that just makes me happy – so bright, so sunny and so delicate! This recipe is a great illustration of subtle umami flavours, rather than the punchy tomato, ham and cheese recipes that commonly feature when capturing savoury deliciousness. You can replace the millet with brown rice or any wholegrain of your choice.

SUNSHINE LAKSA WITH CRAB & SNOW PEAS

200 g/1 cup millet

1 tablespoon vegetable oil

2 x 400-ml/14-oz. cans coconut milk

500 ml/2 cups chicken stock

500 ml/2 cups water

2 tablespoons fish sauce

5 kaffir lime leaves

1 lemongrass stalk, crushed

freshly squeezed juice of 3 limes

250 g/9 oz. white crab meat

200 g/3 small handfuls mangetout/snow peas, cut on the diagonal into 1-cm/½-in pieces

4 spring onions/scallions, finely chopped

TO SERVE

2 red chillies/chiles, deseeded and finely chopped

1 handful of coriander/ cilantro, chopped

lime wedges

LAKSA PASTE

3 shallots, cut in half

3 garlic cloves

3 red chillies/chiles, (I recommend 1 with the seeds left in and 2 deseeded; leave more with seeds in if you want it hotter)

2 lemongrass stalks, chopped

2.5-cm/1-in. square piece of ginger, roughly chopped

1½ tablespoons any nut or seed butter

2 teaspoons shrimp paste

2 teaspoons curry powder

½ teaspoon salt

1 tablespoon vegetable oil

SERVES 4

Place all the laksa paste ingredients in a small food processor and blitz to a paste.

Cook the millet according to the packet instructions, set aside and leave covered to stay warm.

Heat the oil in a large heavy-based saucepan over a high heat. Add the laksa paste and cook for 1 minute to release all the aromatics.

Add the coconut milk, chicken stock, water, fish sauce, kaffir lime leaves and lemongrass to the pot and bring to the boil for 10 minutes. Remove from the heat and add the lime juice.

Take some warm serving bowls and in the base put 1½ tablespoons of millet, 1½ tablespoons crab meat, one-quarter of the mangetout/snow peas and some spring onions/scallions and ladle over the piping hot broth.

Serve with the red chillies/chiles, coriander/cilantro and lime wedges.

Once you master crafting koftas, the permutations are endless. Traditionally made with lamb, you can literally use any minced/ground meat of your choice and experiment with seasoning. I like to serve these with hot sauce, a good Tzatziki, toasted flat breads or rice and a fresh-tasting chopped salad (little gem hearts, tomatoes, cucumber, red onion and plenty of fresh mint) dressed with olive oil and lemon.

GRILLED LAMB KOFTAS

1 onion
1 green (bell) pepper, deseeded
1 extra large handful of flat-leaf parsley
1 extra large handful of mint, leaves only
2 teaspoons tomato purée/paste
1½ teaspoons ground cumin
1½ teaspoons paprika
1 teaspoon ground cinnamon
1 teaspoon ground allspice
fresh nutmeg
sea salt and freshly ground black pepper
400 g/14 oz. finely minced/ground lamb, pork or turkey
50 g/½ cup minus 1 tablespoon toasted pine nuts, chopped

25 g/2 tablespoons raisins
1 egg yolk
250 g/1½ cups cherry tomatoes
2 red onions, cut into skewerable wedges
2 yellow (bell) peppers cut into squares for skewering
6 rashers/slices smoked bacon, cut into 2.5-cm/1-in. squares
olive oil, for cooking

8–10 long wooden skewers, soaked in water

SERVES 4

Pulse the onion and pepper in a food processor until finely chopped. Remove from processor and squeeze out any liquid through a sieve/strainer. Chop the fresh herbs and place in a large bowl, add the onions, green pepper, tomato purée/paste and spices. Mix thoroughly and season well with a good grating of nutmeg, salt and plenty of freshly ground black pepper.

Add the minced/ground meat, pine nuts, raisins and egg yolk to the paste and mix well. Shape into kofta balls using lightly oiled hands.

Thread the cherry tomatoes, onion, (bell) peppers and bacon on to the prepared skewers, making sure there is a square of bacon on either side of the kofta ball to keep it moist. Drizzle the koftas with a little olive oil and grill, bake or barbecue, until cooked through and nicely browned.

An amazing combination of ingredients, the umami comes from the sweet potato and the smoked mackerel. The grapefruit and fennel add an important and transformative tangy crunch.

SWEET POTATO, SMOKED MACKEREL & GRAPEFRUIT SALAD

4 medium sweet potatoes, washed and cut into large dice

8 garlic cloves, crushed by hand

8 fresh thyme sprigs

4 tablespoons olive oil

sea salt and freshly ground black pepper

4 smoked mackerel fillets, flaked into bite-sized chunks

4 fennel bulbs, thinly sliced

2 pink grapefruit, divided into segments and peeled

1 handful chopped flat-leaf parsley

2 tablespoons red wine vinegar

4 tablespoons olive oil

SERVES 4

Preheat the oven to 180°C (350°F) Gas 4.

Place the sweet potatoes, garlic and thyme onto a roasting tray. Drizzle with the olive oil and season with salt and pepper. Toss to combine and roast for 20–25 minutes. Leave to cool.

Place the mackerel, fennel, grapefruit segments, cooked sweet potatoes and parsley into a large mixing bowl. Drizzle with the red wine vinegar and olive oil and season with salt and pepper. Toss to combine and serve.

This salad is delicious served with some horseradish cream on the side.

SUMAC-ROASTED TOMATOES WITH FETA & WALNUTS

I love sumac for its pink, zingy, heady flavour. It is fantastic with tomatoes and a great complement to the feta, walnuts and mint.

6 ripe plum tomatoes, preferably on the vine
sea salt and freshly ground black pepper
1 tablespoon molasses sugar
olive oil
1 tablespoon sumac
3 thyme sprigs, leaves only

200 g/1½ cups feta cheese, crumbled
1 handful walnuts, roughly chopped
1 handful mint, finely chopped

SERVES 2–3 AS A SIDE

Preheat the oven to 150°C (300°F) Gas 2.

Cut the tomatoes in half lengthways and place on a baking tray. Season each one with salt and pepper and a light sprinkling of sugar. Drizzle with a good glug of oil then sprinkle with thyme leaves.

Place the tomatoes in the preheated oven and slow-roast for 20 minutes until the tomatoes have softened and the sugar has caramelized. While the tomatoes are cooking, mix the feta, walnuts and mint together.

Remove the tomatoes from the oven and scatter over the feta mixture, then return to the oven for a further 10 minutes until the feta and walnuts begin to colour.

ROASTED CORN WITH MANCHEGO & LIME

I first had a version of this moreish side at ABC Kitchen in New York. I love the bright flavours almost as much as I love ABC Kitchen and the adjoining store.

6 corn on the cob/ears of corn, husked
1 tablespoon olive oil
1 large knob/pat of butter
salt and freshly ground black pepper
1 fresh or pickled jalapeño, deseeded, finely chopped

zest and freshly squeezed juice of 2 limes
90 g/1 cup grated/shredded mature/sharp Manchego cheese
bunch of coriander/cilantro, finely chopped

SERVES 4

Preheat the oven to 180°C (350°F) Gas 4.

Wrap the corn in foil and place on a baking sheet. Bake in the oven for 45 minutes, turning them halfway through.

Remove from the oven and leave to cool, then cut the kernels from the cobs/ears.

Heat the oil in a large non-stick pan/skillet and add the kernels. Sauté until heated through and the kernels have charred lightly in spots.

Tip into a serving bowl, add the butter, which will melt nicely, then season with salt and pepper.

Add the jalapeño, lime zest and juice, cheese and the coriander/cilantro and mix well to combine.

This recipe is brilliant for entertaining large groups, especially if you have an open-plan kitchen, as everyone can have a go at stirring the pot (I usually tell people that it's lucky to do so – it always gets them going and saves my arm!). The kale pesto can be made in advance and probably makes a little more than you need, so you can cover the surface in olive oil and keep it in the fridge for a couple of days; it's great on pasta or steamed vegetables. If you like your risotto extra boozy, you can replace some of the stock with some more red wine. For dishes where the wine is a feature it is worth investing in a drinkable wine otherwise you can really taste the tannins in the dish, which is not good.

RICH TOMATO RISOTTO WITH KALE PESTO

40 g/3 tablespoons butter
I onion, very finely chopped
320 g/2 cups plus 2 tablespoons Arborio rice
I large glass full-bodied red wine
I litre/quart hot chicken or vegetable stock (or 2 stock cubes dissolved in I litre/quart boiling water)
I tablespoon sundried tomato purée/paste or Taste #5 Umami Bomba! XXX tomato purée/paste
sea salt and freshly ground black pepper

KALE PESTO
3 large handfuls kale, large stalks removed
I large handful basil
40 g/3 tablespoons pine nuts, toasted
50 g/⅔ cup coarsely grated Parmesan cheese
I garlic clove
2 tablespoons extra virgin olive oil
3 tablespoons olive oil
freshly squeezed juice of ½ lemon and zest of I lemon
salt to taste

MANTECATURA (TO FINISH)
60 g/4 tablespoons cold butter, cut into small cubes
85 g/I heaped cup finely grated Parmesan cheese

SERVES 4

In a heavy-based saucepan, melt the butter and sauté the onion until soft and glassy but not coloured. Add the rice and coat until transparent.

Add the wine and stir until half of it has evaporated. Add a ladleful of the hot stock and simmer and stir. As the stock is absorbed add more stock when necessary, taking care to stir throughout (this releases the starch from the rice and make the risotto extra creamy).

Continue adding ladle after ladle of stock and stirring for about 18 minutes until the rice is soft, tender and creamy, but the grains are still al dente in the centre.

Meanwhile, make the pesto by putting all the ingredients into a food processor and whizzing to a paste. Season to taste.

When the risotto is ready, remove it from heat and beat in the butter and Parmesan cheese (the *mantecatura*). Add the sundried tomato purée/paste or Umami Bomba! XXX tomato purée/paste and adjust the seasoning.

To serve, ladle some risotto onto a plate and top with a generous spoonful of kale pesto.

You can see why this recipe ended up in this chapter. It tastes even better than it looks and is packed with umami from the beet(root), anchovies and Parmesan cheese. When testing this recipe I had just roasted some sweet potatoes and spooned the dressing over those instead of the lettuce; my friend said it was the most colourful meal she had ever eaten and we fantasized about serving this delightful dish with a matcha green tea guacamole (usual recipe for guacamole but with a sprinkling of about half a teaspoon of matcha) and a chopped mango, red onion and coriander/cilantro salsa. Pink, orange, green and yellow – that is about as bright and bold as it gets! For a simpler approach, stick with an iceberg wedge.

BEETROOT CAESAR WEDGE

1 iceberg lettuce
handful of finely chopped chives
1 tablespoon pumpkin seeds, toasted in a dry pan/skillet
extra virgin olive oil
freshly ground black pepper

DRESSING
3 garlic cloves
2 medium beet(root), cooked, peeled and cut into chunks
1 tablespoon Dijon mustard
1 tablespoon white wine vinegar

3 anchovy fillets, in oil, drained (optional)
sea salt and freshly ground black pepper
2 heaped tablespoons mayonnaise
4 tablespoons extra virgin olive oil
1 tablespoon grated Parmesan cheese
dash of Worcestershire sauce
squeeze of fresh lemon juice

SERVES 2

To make the dressing, put the garlic, beetroot, mustard, vinegar, anchovies (if using) and a pinch of salt and pepper in a food processor and blend until smooth. Add the mayonnaise and blend again. Slowly add the oil in a steady stream until the mixture has a thick dressing consistency.

Fold in the Parmesan cheese using a spatula and season with the Worcestershire sauce and lemon juice.

Remove and discard the outer leaves from the lettuce, then cut out 2 large wedges.

Place a lettuce wedge on each plate and spoon the dressing across the middle of the wedges. Sprinkle with the chives and toasted pumpkin seeds. Finish with a drizzle of olive oil and some freshly ground black pepper.

This is a great recipe even though I say so myself! It is all in the title. You will be hard-pushed to find a more super or savoury roast chicken recipe around. To save time you can make the paste in advance and store it covered in the fridge for up to 3 days until ready to use.

SUPER SAVOURY ROAST CHICKEN

1 x 1.5 kg/3¼ lbs.
  free-range chicken
3 onions, quartered
1 rosemary sprig
1 small handful of dried
  mushrooms, such as
  shiitake
6 tablespoons olive oil
sea salt and freshly
  ground black pepper
300 ml/1¼ cups red
  wine
300 ml/1¼ cups water

**SUPER-SAVOURY
PASTE**
1 chicken stock cube
3 garlic cloves (large)
4 sundried tomatoes
1½ tablespoons olive oil
1 tablespoon maple
  syrup
½ tablespoon tomato
  purée/paste
½ tablespoon soy sauce
½ tablespoon fish sauce
1½ tablespoons paprika
½ teaspoon chilli/hot
  red pepper flakes
2 rosemary sprigs
  (leaves only), plus
  extra for garnishing

SERVES 4

Preheat the oven to 200°C (400°F) Gas 6.

Pat the chicken dry with some paper towels.

Place 2 onion quarters, the sprig of rosemary and the dried mushrooms into the cavity of the chicken.

Take the remaining onion quarters and place into a roasting tray to form a trivet (three-pronged stand) and place the chicken on top.

Rub the chicken all over with the olive oil and pour any extra in to the tray – this is necessary in order to create a robust gravy. Season with a sprinkling of sea salt and plenty of freshly ground black pepper. Place in the preheated oven, uncovered, for 20 minutes.

Meanwhile, make the paste by putting all the ingredients into a food processor and blend until smooth.

Mix the paste with the wine and water in a large jug/pitcher.

After 20 minutes, turn down the oven temperature to 180°C (350°F) Gas 4. Remove the tray and pour the paste and wine mixture around the chicken – it is important you don't pour it over the chicken at this stage. Put back into the oven for 50 minutes.

Take the chicken out of the oven again. For a total flavour-bomb attack, carefully baste the chicken with the rich gravy from the roasting tray, spooning it all over the chicken and into every crevice.

Place back in the oven for a final 15 minutes so that the skin takes on all the flavour of the sauce. Ensure the chicken is cooked by inserting a skewer between the leg and breast. If the juices run clear, then it is cooked.

Chicken soup is packed with umami, especially when it's made with carrot and onion. This lovely, lemony version is a variation of the Greek sauce/soup *Avgolemono*; the main difference being that I've removed the egg white and added extra egg yolks for a smooth creamy finish. It's a wonderful pick-me-up if you're feeling under the weather.

LEMON CHICKEN SOUP

1 x 1.4 kg/3 lb. organic or free-range chicken

1 tablespoon sea salt

1 carrot, peeled and quartered

1 leek, cleaned and quartered

1 celery stick

3 garlic cloves

1 teaspoon peppercorns

2 bay leaves

2 tablespoons extra-virgin olive oil

1 onion, finely chopped

140 g/¾ cup Arborio rice or short-grain brown rice

1½ teaspoons dried tarragon

freshly squeezed juice of 3–4 lemons

4 egg yolks

good grinding of black pepper

100 g/2 cups baby spinach, washed and drained

130 g/1 cup frozen peas, thawed

SERVES 6–8

Place the chicken in a large pot, with salt, carrot, leek, celery, garlic, peppercorns, and bay leaves and top with 4.5 litres/4¾ quarts of cold water. Bring to the boil over a medium-high heat, then immediately reduce the heat to a very low simmer. Continue to simmer gently until the chicken is cooked, about 45–60 minutes. Continuously skim off any scum that rises to the surface.

Meanwhile, place a frying pan/skillet over a medium-high heat, add the oil and fry the onion slowly, until translucent and soft. Remove from the heat and set aside.

Once the chicken is cooked, remove it from the broth and set aside to cool. Strain the broth and set aside to cool. Once cooled, skim off the fat which should have risen to the surface and be easy to skim off.

When the chicken is cool enough to handle, pull the meat from the bones and remove and discard the skin. Chop up the meat into bite-sized pieces and place in the fridge until ready to use.

Bring the broth back to a boil and add the rice, onion, and tarragon. Reduce the heat and simmer until the rice is al dente, about 15 minutes. Add the chicken and reduce the heat to a low simmer until chicken is hot. Remove from the heat.

In a bowl, beat the lemon juice and egg yolks. Whisk about a large ladleful of the piping hot broth into the egg mixture to temper it. Pour the now warmed egg mixture back into the soup while constantly whisking to blend and season to taste.

Divide the spinach and peas between the serving bowls and ladle the soup over them. Serve immediately.

I like to cook this Tuscan classic when I am catering for a large gathering – it's a great entertaining dish and the salami adds an additional umami twist. We even had this dish as an alternative to turkey last Christmas. Serve with apple sauce. This recipe foregoes pan juices for a smoke-free kitchen, by placing the pork on a rack and cooking above a roasting tray filled with water. That way all the fat drops into the water and does not smoke. If you are a gravy lover and cannot imagine eating this without it, you can conjure up the Miracle Gravy recipe on page 170 so everyone is satisfied.

SALAMI & CHESTNUT PORCHETTA

5.5 kg/12 lbs. boneless loin of pork, with the belly attached
50 g/3 tablespoons butter

STUFFING

2 onions, roughly chopped
25 g/2 tablespoons butter
300 g/10½ oz. good-quality salami, finely chopped
400 g/3 cups cooked chestnuts, roughly chopped
1 large bunch of sage, leaves only and finely chopped
3 rosemary sprigs, leaves only, finely chopped
1 tablespoon coriander seeds
1 tablespoon fennel seeds
sea salt and freshly ground black pepper

SERVES 12–16

Preheat the oven to 150°C (300°F) Gas 2.

To make the stuffing, put the onions into a food processor and whizz until they are finely chopped. Heat a frying pan/skillet until medium hot, add the butter and, when it's foaming, add the chopped onion and cook for 5 minutes until just softened. Add the salami, chestnuts, sage, rosemary, coriander and fennel seeds and season well with salt and plenty of black pepper. When well combined and all the oil has been absorbed by the chestnuts remove from heat and set aside.

Lay the pork, flesh-side up, on a chopping board with the belly flap away from you.

With a sharp knife, cut down the centre of the loin, almost cutting all the way through, then press to open it out flat like a book.

Season with salt and black pepper then spoon and spread the stuffing along the loin.

Roll up the pork with the skin on the outside and secure with cook's string at intervals of 2.5 cm/1 in. Dry the skin well with paper towels and rub the rest of the butter over the top and season with sea salt and black pepper.

Transfer to an oven rack and place a roasting tray of cold water on the shelf underneath to catch the dripping fat. Slow roast for 5 hours. The crackling should be crisp and the pork very tender and succulent.

Leave to rest for at least 20 minutes before carving into thick slices.

GARLIC, CHILLI & PARSLEY PRAWNS

I made this recipe by accident – don't ask how, but the Mediterranean technique and flavours along with a hint of oriental fish sauce keeps people guessing as to how a classic combination of garlic, white wine, tomato and parsley can taste this good. This is also amazing on pasta or spooned over a simple saffron risotto.

I whole head of garlic, thinly sliced
I fresh red chilli/chile (with seeds), finely chopped
4 tablespoons olive oil, plus a splash
500 g/1 lb. 2 oz. fresh prawns/shrimp, heads, tails and shells on
I tablespoon fish sauce, plus an extra splash

100 ml/7 tablespoons dry white wine
freshly ground black pepper
50 g/3 tablespoons butter, at room temperature
I teaspoon tomato purée/paste
I large handful flat-leaf parsley, finely chopped

SERVES 2

Heat half the garlic and chilli/chile in a large frying pan/skillet with some olive oil.

Add the whole prawns/shrimp with I tablespoon fish sauce, half the white wine, and lots of freshly ground black pepper. Stir frequently and allow the prawns/shrimp to cook. They will go from grey to pink in about 2–3 minutes.

Remove the prawns/shrimp from the pan/skillet and take the pan off the heat. Remove the heads and shells to leave you with just the juicy, pink flesh.

Put the pan/skillet back onto a high heat, with a small splash of oil and the rest of the garlic and chilli. When the garlic begins to colour, deglaze the pan/skillet with the remaining white wine and, when this begins to evaporate, toss the peeled prawns/shrimp back into the pan with the butter, a small splash of fish sauce and the tomato purée/paste. Shake and toss well until this glossy sauce coats all the prawns/shrimp.

Take the pan/skillet off the heat and finish by tossing through lots of fresh parsley. Serve immediately.

MONKFISH WITH MANGO & AVOCADO SALSA

This dish certainly lives up to the chapter name. You can replace the monkfish with any sustainable meaty white fish fillet and substitute the mango for ripe strawberries (change the herbs to basil and parsley if you do, though). The umami comes from the Worcestershire sauce; play around with the levels of lemon and balsamic vinegar, but be careful to keep the Worcestershire sauce level above that of lemon or balsamic or you will lose all the umami.

350–400 g/12½–14 oz. monkfish tail, trimmed
sea salt and freshly ground black pepper
squeeze of lemon juice
drizzle of olive oil

MANGO SALSA
8 tablespoons extra virgin olive oil
good squeeze of lemon juice, to taste

I tablespoon Worcestershire sauce
splash of balsamic vinegar
2 handfuls chopped coriander/cilantro
I handful chopped mint
I large ripe but firm mango, peeled, stoned/pitted, and cubed
I large avocado, peeled, stoned/pitted, and cubed

SERVES 2

Preheat the oven to 180°C (350°F) Gas 4. Line an ovenproof dish with baking parchment.

Cut the monkfish into 4 medallions, each about 1.5-cm/¾-in. thick (ask the fishmonger to do this for you). Place the monkfish in the dish, season with salt and pepper and add a squeeze of lemon juice. Drizzle with olive oil and bake for 15 minutes or until the fish is cooked through.

While the fish is cooking, prepare the salsa: mix the oil, lemon juice, Worcestershire sauce, balsamic vinegar and herbs. Season with salt and pepper, then stir in the mango and avocado cubes.

Place 2 monkfish medallions on each plate, spoon over salsa and plenty of the dressing from the bottom of the bowl.

This celebrated dish is all about the power of umami. Created by my father in 1984, Carciofo Santini is his most famous creation, and people come from all over the world to eat this signature dish at Santini – our family restaurant in London. The rich sauce is also served with homemade pappardelle which was Frank Sinatra's favourite Santini dish. As these artichokes take some time to cook, they are best prepared in advance; they can be reheated gently, with a ladleful of stock if necessary.

GINO SANTIN'S CARCIOFO SANTINI
(ARTICHOKE WITH A BIG HEART)

4 globe artichokes

2 vegetable stock cubes, crumbled

2 handfuls flat-leaf parsley, finely chopped

6 garlic cloves, finely chopped

100 g/1½ cups Parmesan cheese, finely grated

100 g/1¾ cups dried breadcrumbs

sea salt and freshly ground black pepper

6 tablespoons extra virgin olive oil

1 litre/quart vegetable stock, hot

SERVES 4

Prepare the artichokes by flattening the top and cutting the sharp points off the leaves. Remove the stalks and any tough, shabby-looking outer leaves (these can be used in the sauce below).

Rub the stock cubes, parsley, garlic, cheese, breadcrumbs, salt and pepper together into a powder with your fingers (as if you were making a crumble topping).

Heat 4 tablespoons of the oil in the base of a frying pan/skillet with a lid. When hot but not spitting, add the artichokes and brown the bottoms, then turn to brown the tops. They will begin to caramelize but do not worry, it is important that they do as this will add to the flavour – as long as you don't let them burn.

Once browned, spread open the leaves of the artichokes and press the powder down into the crevices as far as you can, keeping some back for later. Turn the artichokes upside down (some of the mixture might fall into the bottom of the pan, but this will help the sauce), set upright again and sprinkle with the remaining powder.

Drizzle with more olive oil and add 500 ml/ 2 cups of the stock. Bring to the boil and leave to reduce over a low heat. Keep adding stock as the sauce reduces, until the artichokes are tender and the sauce thickens. Cook over a low heat, with the lid on, for about 1–1¼ hours. Check often to make sure the artichokes don't catch on the bottom and add a ladleful of stock as necessary. Serve the artichokes hot, pouring the pan juices over them.

Packed with flavours and aromatics that are typical of the Mediterranean and Middle East regions, this is a truly brilliant recipe and once you have mastered it, you will make it with your eyes closed.

This is a typically Venetian dish and one my father taught me as a child. It is such a perfect example of umami alchemy – the magic of this dish can be tasted in between the sweet onion and the super-savoury anchovies.

HABIBI CHICKEN

2 unwaxed lemons, thinly sliced into rounds
8 chicken thigh fillets, bone in, skin on
1 head of garlic, cloves separated, unpeeled
200 g/1½ cups olives (mixed colours)
150 ml/½ cup plus 2 tablespoons prepared chicken stock
1 tablespoon harissa paste
100 g/7 tablespoons tomato purée/paste
1 tablespoon dark brown sugar
1 teaspoon dried cumin seeds
sea salt and freshly ground black pepper
500 g/3 cups cherry tomatoes on the vine
1 handful fresh mint, roughly chopped

SERVES 4

Preheat the oven to 180°C (350°F) Gas 4.

Place the slices of lemon in a single layer in a large roasting tray. Place the chicken pieces on top of the lemon slices. Scatter over the garlic cloves and olives.

In a measuring jug/pitcher, combine the stock, harissa paste, tomato purée/paste, sugar and cumin seeds. Pour the liquid over the chicken and season with salt and freshly ground black pepper. Cover the tray well with aluminium foil and roast in the preheated oven for 1 hour.

Increase the oven temperature to 200°C (400°F) and remove the chicken. Give everything a gentle stir and add the tomatoes on the vine, placing them carefully around the chicken pieces. Return to the oven and roast for a further 25–35 minutes until the chicken is cooked through and the skin is crisp and golden.

Top with the fresh mint.

BIGOLI IN SALSA

2 tablespoons olive oil
2 very large onions, thinly sliced
200 g/7 oz. salted anchovy fillets in olive oil, drained
freshly ground black pepper
400 g/14 oz. bigoli pasta (thick, Venetian spaghetti-
style pasta with a tiny hole running through) or thick spaghetti
freshly grated truffle or a few drops of truffle oil (optional)

SERVES 4

Heat the olive oil in a heavy-based frying pan/skillet. Add the onions and cook until golden.

Add the anchovies and a good grinding of black pepper and stir until the anchovies have dissolved into the softened onions. Remove from the heat.

Cook the pasta according to the packet instructions in plenty of salted boiling water. Drain and toss into the pan with the sauce, making sure to coat the pasta well.

If you want you can finish with some freshly grated truffle or a couple of drops of truffle oil. Serve immediately.

photo of Bigoli in Salsa: page 115 (top)

This recipe epitomizes Heady and Daring, and it is wonderfully creamy and super-indulgent. It makes a fantastic alternative to canapés at a drinks party – you can make a big pot and serve it on little plates that get passed around. Serve with any remaining chilled Champagne. If you are feeling utterly indulgent, you could use caviar instead of bottarga.

CHAMPAGNE & PARMESAN RISOTTO WITH BOTTARGA

1 onion, very finely chopped in a food processor to the size of the grains of rice

40 g/3 tablespoons butter or 3 tablespoons olive oil

320 g/1¾ cups Arborio rice (1 fistful per person plus 2 for the pot)

275 ml/1 cup plus 2 tablespoons Champagne

850 ml/3½ cups hot chicken or vegetable stock, or 2 stock cubes dissolved in 1 litre/ quart of boiling water

salt flakes and freshly ground black pepper

bottarga, either shavings or grated

MANTECATURA (TO FINISH)

60 g/4 tablespoons cold butter, cut into small cubes

85 g/1¼ cups finely grated Parmesan cheese

SERVES 4

Prepare both the butter and the cheese for the *mantecatura* and keep in the fridge until needed at the end.

In a large heavy-based saucepan, sauté the onion in the butter or olive oil until soft.

Add the rice and stir until translucent and glassy. Do not allow the butter to overheat or any of the ingredients to brown. Add 125 ml/½ cup Champagne and stir well until it has evaporated.

Add a ladleful of hot stock and simmer, stirring all the time with a wooden spoon. As the stock is absorbed, continue to add a ladleful of stock at a time, still stirring.

When you run out of stock, add the remaining Champagne. Remember, the more you stir, the creamier the risotto! When all the stock and Champagne has been incorporated, the rice should be soft on the outside with a firm centre and the risotto should be nice and creamy. This will take about 18 minutes.

Remove the pan from the heat and beat in the butter and Parmesan (the *mantecatura*). Adjust the seasoning and top with bottarga.

TUNA MELT WITH BANANA

Sound nuts? Well you'd be nuts not to try this…

110 g/⅔ cup plus
  1 tablespoon canned tuna
2 tablespoons mayonnaise
100 g/1 packed cup plus
  1 tablespoon
  grated/shredded
  mature/sharp Cheddar
  cheese
2 teaspoons Taste #5
  Umami Bomb/Paste
  Original Recipe
freshly squeezed juice
  of ½ lemon
2 tablespoons
  coriander/cilantro,
  finely chopped
freshly ground black pepper
2 thick slices sourdough
  bread
butter
1 small red onion, cut in
  half and finely sliced
1 banana, sliced diagonally

SERVES 1

Preheat the grill/broiler to the highest setting.

In a medium bowl, mix together the tuna, mayonnaise, most of the Cheddar cheese (leaving some to sprinkle on top), Umami Bomb/Paste, lemon juice and coriander/cilantro and season with plenty of freshly ground black pepper.

Place a large frying pan/skillet over a medium-high heat. Butter one side of each slice of bread and place the bread, buttered-side down, in the pan/skillet. Top with slices of onion and banana.

Cook until the bottom of the bread is well toasted. Transfer slices of bread, toasted-side down, to a baking sheet and top with the tuna mixture and a sprinkling of extra Cheddar. Put under the preheated grill/broiler for around 5 minutes until the topping is golden and bubbling. Serve immediately.

This recipe was a last-minute addition to the book, made after dining with Con and Simon who photographed and styled this book so beautifully. The three of us met at chef and master-flavourists Ignacio Mattos's restaurant Estela in New York. This light but umami-packed salad was, for me, the culinary highlight of the dinner and we all agreed it had to go into the book. I have adapted Ignacio's recipe slightly (the original can be found online) and added sumac, apricots and mint to make it even more heady and daring. I hope you love it as much as we did. The trick here is to toast the breadcrumbs and walnuts until really flavoursome and dark brown.

STARLIGHT SALAD WITH SUMAC, APRICOTS & MINT

60 g/1 cup coarse brown breadcrumbs
6 tablespoons olive oil
sea salt and freshly ground black pepper
4 anchovy fillets in oil, drained and finely chopped
1 garlic clove, finely grated
2 tablespoons red wine vinegar
5 dried apricots, chopped into small pieces
50 g/⅓ cup walnut halves, roughly chopped and toasted
120 g/1 cup aged Pecorino cheese or aged Parmesan cheese, cut into 0.5-cm/¼-in. cubes

4 chicory/endives, sliced crossways, into 2-cm/¾-in. thick pieces
freshly squeezed juice and zest of 1 orange
1 tablespoon white balsamic vinegar or white wine vinegar
handful finely chopped mint
3 teaspoons sumac

SERVES 4

Preheat the oven to 180°C (350°F) Gas 4.

Toss the breadcrumbs with 2 tablespoons of the oil and place on a baking sheet. Season generously with salt. Bake in the preheated oven until golden brown, about 12–15 minutes, tossing occasionally. Set aside to cool.

Mix the anchovies, garlic, red wine vinegar and remaining olive oil in a medium bowl and season with salt and pepper. Add the apricots, toasted walnuts, breadcrumbs and Pecorino or Parmesan cubes and toss to combine.

In another large bowl, toss the chicory/endives with the orange juice and zest, vinegar and mint. Sprinkle with sumac and season with salt and pepper.

To serve, divide the walnut mixture among the plates and top with the chicory/endive salad.

This is a hybrid of Boston Baked Beans and Campfire Chilli Con Carne complete with cowboy coffee and a Mexican chocolate twist. I have replaced the kidney beans (not my favourite) with my preferred good, honest haricot/navy beans. This recipe makes lots and you will be glad it does as it gets better the day after. With regard to heat, it obviously ain't a Chilli Con Carne if it ain't hot, but on the other hand most small children can't handle super hot, so adjust the amount of chilli accordingly.

BOSTON CHILLI CON CARNE

3 tablespoons olive oil

1 large onion, finely chopped

1 carrot, finely diced

2 celery stalks, finely diced

4 garlic cloves, finely chopped

1 kg/2¼ lbs. minced/ground beef

8 rashers/slices smoked streaky/fatty bacon, cut into small strips

2 teaspoons ground cumin

1 teaspoon hot chilli powder

½–1 dried chipotle chilli, crumbled (optional)

2 teaspoons smoked paprika

1 cinnamon stick

3 teaspoons dried oregano

2 bay leaves

2 red (bell) peppers, cut into strips

2 x 400-g/14-oz. cans chopped tomatoes

4 tablespoons double concentrated tomato purée/paste

300 ml/1¼ cups dark beer

100 ml/7 tablespoons strong coffee

2 beef stock cubes

dash of Nam Pla fish sauce

½ tablespoon blackstrap molasses or ½ tablespoon dark muscovado sugar

sea salt and freshly ground black pepper

2 x 400-g/14-oz. cans haricot/navy beans, drained and rinsed

25 g/1 oz. dark/bittersweet chocolate (70% cocoa solids)

TO SERVE

handful of coriander/cilantro, roughly chopped

1 tablespoon sliced jalapeño peppers in brine, drained and finely chopped

juice of ½ lime

sour cream

blue tortilla chips

SERVES 4–6

Preheat the oven to 180°C (350°F) Gas 4.

In a large ovenproof frying pan/skillet, heat the oil over a low heat and fry the onion, carrot, celery and garlic for about 10 minutes until the onion is soft and translucent but not browned.

Turn the heat to high and add the minced/ground beef and bacon strips and fry until the beef is browned all over.

Stir in the spices and herbs (note that half a chipotle chilli, deseeded, will give you the flavour but not the heat) and cook for a further 2–3 minutes, then add the red (bell) peppers.

Stir in the tomatoes, tomato purée/paste, beer, coffee, stock cubes, fish sauce, molasses and season with salt and pepper to taste.

Finally add the beans then cover and transfer the pan to the preheated oven for 30–40 minutes.

Remove from the oven and stir in the chocolate. Continue stirring until the chocolate has melted.

For the garnish, mix the chopped coriander/cilantro and jalapeño peppers together with the lime juice.

Serve the chilli topped with the with jalapeño mixture, sour cream and tortilla chips.

Umami fills the intensely savoury things that make you go 'mmmmm', and this platter is full of 'mmmmm'. Home picnics are great — there's no washing up and everybody can tuck in straight away. To make more of a meal of it, prepare a simple tomato, onion and basil salad and bolster up the picnic with some salami, bresaola, extra cheeses, such as Pecorino and Gorgonzola, and add walnuts, mascarpone and honey on the side…

UMAMI PICNIC

1 tube Taste #5 Umami Bomb/Paste Original Recipe
8 salted anchovies in oil
truffle oil
12 sundried tomatoes
12 bite-sized chunks Parmesan cheese
4 tablespoons marinated green olives
4 tablespoons marinated black olives
1 jar of marinated mushrooms in oil
1 jar of artichoke pieces in oil
12 slices of Prosciutto di Parma

TO SERVE
extra virgin olive oil
aged balsamic vinegar
mixed Italian breads

SERVES 4–6

Squeeze out about a tablespoon of the Umami Bomb/Paste and place the tube onto a wooden serving board.

Drizzle the anchovies with the truffle oil.

Arrange these and all the other platter ingredients neatly onto the serving board. Be careful not to overfill the platter as it will begin to look messy.

Give each person a ramekin with a drizzle of olive oil and a splash of balsamic vinegar and let everybody dig in!

photo of Umami Picnic: pages 126–127

I have long been a fan of roasting kale, but it has become increasingly popular over the last year or so, mainly due to kale being low in fat and calories and very high in nutrients. Lots of shops are now selling pre-packed kale chips, but it is much cheaper just to make your own at home – and very easy too.

KALE CHIPS WITH NUTRITIONAL YEAST

400 g/14 oz. kale
2 tablespoons olive oil
1 tablespoon soy sauce
1 tablespoon maple syrup
freshly squeezed juice of
  ½ lemon
¼ teaspoon cayenne pepper
1 tablespoon nutritional
  yeast or a sprinkling of
  Taste #5 Umami Rush or
  Taste #5 Umami Pepper

SERVES 4–6
AS A SNACK

Preheat the oven to 180°C (350°F) Gas 4.

Rinse the kale and dry thoroughly. Remove and discard the thick stalks and roughly chop the leaves. Pat the leaves dry again.

Mix the olive oil, soy sauce, maple syrup, lemon and cayenne pepper together in a bowl. Toss the kale together with olive oil mixture.

Spread onto a baking sheet and sprinkle with nutritional yeast, Umami Rush or Umami Pepper.

Bake for 15–20 minutes, stirring every 5 minutes, until the leaves are crisp with slightly browned edges.

SPIKED TOMATOES

A recipe stolen from a fabulously glamorous woman called Anna, who is not ashamed to admit that this is the only meal she knows how to cook. Famed for lighting a cigarette at a very formal dinner party as other guests were enjoying their main courses and then uttering the now immortalized words 'Do you mind not eating while I smoke?', Anna makes this potent dish either with Umami Vodka (yes it exists) or Hendrick's Gin. Ordinary vodka works well too.

800 g/1¾ lbs. sweet cherry tomatoes
500 ml/2 cups vodka or gin
½ teaspoon sugar

Umami Salt (see page 171), or Taste #5 Umami Rush, to serve

SERVES 10–16 AS A CANAPÉ

With a cocktail stick/toothpick, poke a hole through the centre of each tomato and transfer the tomatoes to a large bowl.

Add the vodka or gin and sugar to the tomatoes and cover with clingfilm/plastic wrap. Place in the fridge and marinate for 24 hours.

Drain the tomatoes and place in a serving bowl.

Place the umami salt or Umami Rush in small serving bowls and cocktail sticks/toothpicks in small containers so you can dip the tomatoes. Serve at once.

WALNUT BAGNA CAUDA

This creamy, savoury dip is the ultimate treat for any self-respecting crudité. Although making it is not a quick process, it is well worth waiting for! Walnuts can be omitted for those of you who prefer to keep it simple.

200 g/7 oz. garlic, thinly sliced
200 g/7 oz. anchovies in oil, rinsed and drained
1 handful finely chopped walnuts
400 g/3½ sticks unsalted butter

splash of double/heavy cream
twist of black pepper
mixed vegetable crudité, to serve

SERVES 6–8

Half-fill a saucepan with water and bring to the boil. Find a Pyrex bowl, both large enough to hold all of your ingredients, and the right size to sit over your saucepan without falling in or sticking out too much.

Place the garlic in the bottom of the bowl, top with anchovies and walnuts and finally the butter and a splash of cream. Lower the heat and leave to simmer gently for about 1 hour until all the ingredients have dissolved into a seriously tasty sauce. Don't be tempted to increase the temperature here – heating it quickly will cause the mixture to split permanently. Season with a twist of black pepper.

This simple dish was developed by my friend and mentor celebrity chef Nobu Matsuhisa, with whom I have collaborated on a miso-based vegetarian version of my umami paste. This recipe, however, uses my original tomato umami paste. A stunning recipe for mussels, this tastes unlike any other mussel recipe I have ever tasted, and uses our original Umami Bomb/Paste. Serve with plenty of chopped fresh herbs, more sake and some crusty bread to mop up the juices.

SAKE MUSSELS

1 kg/2 lb. 3 oz. cultivated mussels, rinsed and scrubbed
250 ml/1 cup sake
2 tablespoons Taste #5 Umami Bomb/Paste Original Recipe
4 teaspoons finely chopped garlic
4 teaspoons finely chopped fresh ginger
2 large, ripe tomatoes, chopped
fresh flat-leaf parsley and chives, chopped, to serve

SERVES 2

Make sure the mussels are clean and any tendrils ('beards') are removed from the sides of the shells. Discard any that are open or open when tapped.

Mix the sake with the Umami Bomb/Paste, garlic, and ginger in a small bowl.

Place a large saucepan with a tight-fitting lid over a high heat. When hot, add the mussels, sake mixture and tomatoes and cover tightly with the lid. Steam for 3–4 minutes.

When the mussels are cooked, the shells should have opened. Discard any mussels that are still closed.

Place the mussels and sauce in a serving bowl and scatter with parsley and chives.

I love spicy tuna rolls – they are always my favourite sushi order. This recipe deconstructs that concept to make a sophisticated and different appetizer or a healthful meal in a bowl. If you like it really spicy, add a pinch of Shichimi Togarashi (Japanese 7 Spice Powder). All the ingredients can be prepped in advance so all you have to do is assemble it before serving, making it the perfect dish for a sexy dinner date. Serve with chilled Champagne, sake or vodka; you can leave out the spring onion/scallion if you are not that close. Sweeten the savoury by following it with some fresh strawberries and some good-quality dark chocolates…

SPICY TUNA AND BLACK RICE BOWL

240 g/1 cup plus 3 tablespoons black rice
60 g/4 tablespoons wild rice
1 tablespoon sesame oil
560 g/1¼ lbs. fresh, sushi-grade tuna, chopped into 1 cm/½ in. cubes
½ cucumber, deseeded and chopped into 1 cm/½ in. cubes
1 ripe but firm avocado, chopped into 1 cm/½ in. cubes
6 spring onions/scallions, finely sliced
2.5-cm/1-in. piece fresh ginger, finely grated
2 tablespoons soy sauce
4 sheets nori
furikake seasoning or toasted sesame seeds
2–4 limes, to serve

SPICY MAYONNAISE
4 tablespoons mayonnaise (preferably Japanese mayonnaise if you can find it)
½ teaspoon tomato ketchup
Sriracha hot sauce or Tabasco, to taste

SERVES 4 AS A MAIN, 8 AS AN APPETIZER

Cook the rices together in a large pot of boiling salted water until tender but still al dente with a nice bite but not raw. This should take about 35 minutes. Drain well. Place in a bowl and mix in the sesame oil while the rice is still hot. Set aside to cool.

To make the tuna mixture, combine the tuna, cucumber, avocado, spring onions/scallions, ginger and soy sauce.

Make the spicy mayonnaise sauce by mixing the mayonnaise and ketchup with as much Sriracha or Tabasco sauce as you can handle.

Prepare the nori garnish by folding each sheet of nori over four times, and then slicing it into thin shreds.

Assemble the dish. For each person, spoon about 1–2 tablespoons (if serving as an appetizer), or 2–3 tablespoons (if serving as a main) of rice into a flat bowl. Top with a generous spoonful of the tuna mixture, then gently top with a small spoonful of spicy mayonnaise. Generously scatter nori shreds and a sprinkle of furikake seasoning (or toasted sesame seeds). Serve with half a lime per person.

All the ingredients of this classic (except the beef) can be pre-prepared, making it very quick to assemble. It goes very well with a glass of good velvety red wine and a hot dessert to follow; try keeping the wine theme going by serving the Rich Chocolate Mulled Wine and Fig & Walnut Biscotti on page 165 afterwards.

STEAK TARTARE

500 g/1 lb. 2 oz. fillet of beef, finely chopped
1½ tablespoons chopped gherkins/pickled cucumbers
3 tablespoons finely chopped flat-leaf parsley
1½ tablespoons chopped capers
1½ tablespoons finely chopped shallot
3 tablespoons tomato ketchup
3 teaspoons Worcestershire sauce
1 tablespoon Dijon mustard
generous splash of Tabasco
1 tablespoon olive oil, plus extra for drizzling
salt flakes and freshly ground black pepper
4 egg yolks
hot sourdough toast, to serve

SERVES 4

Combine all the ingredients except the egg yolks.

Divide the mixture between 4 chilled plates and make a well in the middle for the whole egg yolk.

Put the egg yolks in the wells.

Lightly drizzle the plate with olive oil, salt flakes and freshly ground black pepper. Serve immediately with hot sourdough toast.

I first tried aubergine/eggplant with blackstrap molasses on the beach in Spain and remember it fondly. Being the greedy girl that I am, I have taken this dish one step further, creating a divine Mediterranean/Middle Eastern mix. Serve with good crusty bread or crispy flatbread.

RICOTTA, AUBERGINE, MOLASSES AND CRUMBLED PROSCIUTTO

4 large aubergines/ eggplants
8 slices Prosciutto
olive oil, for frying
sea salt and freshly ground black pepper
500 g/1 lb. 2 oz. quality fresh ricotta cheese
1 handful black olives, stoned/pitted and quartered
blackstrap molasses
sprinkling of flat-leaf parsley, finely chopped, to garnish
zest of 1 lemon, grated
extra virgin olive oil, for drizzling

SERVES 4

Preheat the grill/broiler to high.

Top and tail each aubergine/eggplant, then stand it up vertically and cut the 4 sides (skin on) of each one off, making each side around 2 cm/¾ in. thick. (You can keep the cores of the aubergine/eggplant to roast and make into a dip, by adding to blender with olive oil, lemon, salt and pepper and a dollop of tahini).

Halve each slice of aubergine/eggplant horizontally, then slice these into 1-cm/½-in. batons. Place the aubergine/eggplant batons into a colander, sprinkle with approximately 2 tablespoons sea salt and mix thoroughly. Place something very heavy over the aubergines/eggplants, press down and then put the colander into a larger bowl or pan to catch the juices. Leave for at least 30 minutes, so all the bitter juices run out.

While you wait, grill the Prosciutto until golden and very crispy.

Remove the aubergine/eggplant batons from the colander, rinse well and squeeze out any excess liquid. Dry well with paper towels.

In a large saucepan, shallow-fry the aubergine/ eggplant batons in batches until golden and slightly chewy. Remove and transfer to a baking tray covered with paper towels. Season with just black pepper (they will probably be salty enough). Keep warm in a low oven while you fry the rest.

Roughly spread the ricotta on a large serving dish and scatter the aubergine/eggplant and olive pieces on top.

Drizzle with a little molasses and top with the Prosciutto, crumbled in your hands. Combine the parsley and lemon zest together and scatter over the top, with a good twist of black pepper and a drizzle of extra virgin olive oil.

This is one of those OMG dishes and is a real show-stopper, especially if you are generous with the brandy. I like to serve it with fluffy basmati rice to which I add 3 cardamom pods while the rice is steaming to make it extra fragrant.

ROAST CHICKEN WITH POMEGRANATE, PANCETTA AND BRANDY

3 tablespoons olive oil
1 medium chicken, jointed
  into 8 pieces by a butcher
3 shallots (2 quartered,
  1 chopped finely)
1 bunch fresh sage
4 garlic cloves
30 g/1 cup dried porcini
  mushrooms, soaked in
  250 ml/1 cup of boiling
  water, drained and
  chopped (reserve the
  soaking liquid)
4 medium pomegranates
25 g/2 tablespoons butter
100 g/3½ oz. pancetta
generous splash of brandy
250 ml/1 cup double/heavy
  cream
sea salt and freshly ground
  black pepper
basmati rice, to serve

SERVES 4

Preheat the oven to 180°C (350°F) Gas 4.

Heat the olive oil in a cast-iron casserole dish over a medium-high heat. Add the chicken and brown on all sides. Season well with salt and pepper.

Once browned, remove from the heat. Add the quartered shallots, half the sage, the garlic, and the reserved liquid from the mushrooms (about 250 ml/1 cup). Replace the chicken, cover with a tight-fitting lid and roast in the preheated oven for 1 hour.

Meanwhile, deseed the pomegranates by slicing them in half and bashing them with a wooden spoon over a bowl so that the seeds fall out. Crush the seeds slightly with a potato masher to release their juices.

Take out the chicken and pour the pomegranate juices into the pan, reserving the seeds for later. Pop the chicken back into the oven.

Start making the sauce. Heat the butter in a medium saucepan over a medium heat. Once it has melted, add the chopped shallot and cook until translucent. Add the mushrooms, the rest of the sage and the pancetta and cook until the pancetta begins to crisp and the fat melts.

Once the chicken is cooked, pour off its sauce into the mushroom pan. Cover the chicken with foil to keep it warm.

Add the brandy and the double/heavy cream to the sauce. Simmer until the sauce has reduced enough to coat the back of a spoon, then pour it back over the chicken, sprinkle with the reserved pomegranate seeds, and serve immediately with bowls of hot basmati rice.

This old classic is a sexy dish for a hot date. Sadly one half lobster is not quite enough but two is a little too much! Serve with green salad and crisp sourdough toasts and plenty of Champagne.

LOBSTER THERMIDOR

1 x 750 g/1⅔ lbs. lobster,
   cooked
30 g/2 tablespoons butter
1 shallot, finely chopped
250 ml/1 cup fresh fish
   stock
60 ml/¼ cup Vermouth
100 ml/7 tablespoons
   double/heavy cream
45 g/generous ½ cup
   Parmesan cheese, grated
½ teaspoon Dijon mustard
2 tablespoons chopped
   flat-leaf parsley
freshly squeezed juice
   of ½ lemon
sea salt and freshly ground
   black pepper

SERVES 2

Slice the lobster in half from head to tail. Remove the meat from the claws, tail and head. Cut the lobster meat into 2.5 cm/1 in. pieces and place it back in the shell, making sure both halves get an equal amount of claw meat.

For the sauce, melt the butter in a pan, add the shallot and cook on a low-medium heat until glassy. Add the fish stock, Vermouth and double/heavy cream and bring to the boil. Reduce by about half until thick and creamy. Add two-thirds of the Parmesan cheese and the mustard, parsley, lemon juice and seasoning.

Preheat the grill/broiler and spoon the sauce over the lobster meat. Sprinkle with the rest of the grated Parmesan cheese. Place the lobster halves under the pre-heated grill/broiler for 3–4 minutes until golden brown and the lobster is cooked but not chewy.

These curious armadillo-like potatoes are a Scandinavian twist on the roast and jacket potato, providing buttery, fluffy centres with crisp crunchy edges. With the addition of cream, Parmesan cheese and truffles, I've umamified these little critters by adding a dauphenois-y twist into the mix. Serve with grills and simple roasts for mouth-watering results.

FONDANT HASSELBACK POTATOES

750 g/1⅔ lbs. medium waxy potatoes, skin-on (8–9 potatoes)
3 tablespoons olive oil
45 g/3 tablespoons butter
sea salt and freshly ground black pepper
1 rosemary sprig
1 thyme sprig
200 ml/¾ cup plus 2 tablespoons double/heavy cream
2–3 teaspoons truffle paste or mushroom and truffle paste
2 garlic cloves, crushed

2 anchovies, finely chopped
50 g/generous ½ cup Parmesan cheese finely grated

TO SERVE
seasonal fresh black or white truffles or a drizzle of truffle oil (or both)

SERVES 4

Preheat the oven to 200°C (400°F) Gas 6.

Using a small knife, cut deep incisions across each potato (about three quarters of the way through) at intervals of approximately 3-mm/⅛-in. Be careful not to cut all the way through. I find that the best way to do this is to place the potatoes in the bowl of a wooden spoon.

Put the oil and butter in a large, ovenproof sauté pan/skillet over a medium heat. Once the butter has melted and began to foam, add the potatoes cut-side down in one layer. Fry gently until the cut sides are golden brown. Turn the potatoes over and fry again until the other sides are golden brown, basting throughout so the butter goes down into the cracks of the potatoes.

Add the rosemary and thyme to the pan, season the potatoes with salt and pepper and transfer to the preheated oven for about 40–50 minutes.

Meanwhile, in a small saucepan, heat the cream with the truffle paste (or truffle and mushroom paste), garlic, anchovies and three-quarters of the Parmesan cheese and reduce by about a third.

Remove the potatoes from the oven and pour the cream around the potatoes, taking care not to pour it directly over them. Sprinkle the remaining Parmesan cheese over the potatoes.

Return the pan/skillet to the oven for 10 minutes until the cream is bubbling and the Parmesan cheese has melted.

Remove from the oven and generously grate all over with truffle or drizzle with truffle oil (or both) just before serving.

A family favourite in the summer, I like to serve this with a big lemony salad, plenty of fluffy basmati rice and a good dollop of harissa yogurt, which I make by stirring harissa paste and freshly chopped mint into Greek-style yogurt. Again, this is very easy entertaining food, as everything except the rice and grilling the lamb can be prepared in advance.

BUTTERFLIED LAMB WITH MINT AND PINK PEPPERCORN CHERMOULA

I leg of lamb, about 2 kg/4½ lbs., boned and butterflied

MARINADE
5 garlic cloves, crushed
3 sprigs rosemary, leaves only
3 tablespoons olive oil
2 tablespoons freshly squeezed lemon juice
freshly ground black pepper
I teaspoon sea salt

CHERMOULA
2 garlic cloves
2 teaspoons coriander seeds
2 teaspoons fennel seeds
6 heaped teaspoons ground cumin

2 tablespoons pink peppercorns
salt flakes and freshly ground black pepper
4 large handfuls of flat-leaf parsley, chopped
2 large handful of mint
I tablespoon dried edible rose petals, finely chopped (optional)
300 ml/1¼ cups extra virgin olive oil
freshly squeezed juice of 3 lemons
3 tablespoons soy sauce
3 tablespoons Worcestershire sauce

SERVES 6

To make the marinade, place the garlic, rosemary leaves, oil, lemon juice, salt and pepper in a blender and pulse until roughly chopped enough to rub into the meat.

Place the meat on a chopping board and score it with a knife on both sides so the marinade sinks in well. Rub the marinade into the meat on both sides making sure it is well coated and place in a shallow dish. Cover with clingfilm/plastic wrap and leave to marinate in the fridge overnight.

To make the chermoula, pound the garlic, coriander and fennel seeds, cumin, pink peppercorns and a couple of pinches of salt flakes and a good grinding of pepper into a paste.

Add the parsley, mint and rose petals, and continue to pound. Gradually add the oil, lemon juice, soy sauce and Worcestershire sauce to produce a consistency somewhere between a pesto and a dressing. Season to taste with more salt and pepper if it needs it.

To cook the lamb, pre-heat a grill/broiler or barbecue to a high heat. Remove the meat from the marinade and season with a little salt and pepper. Place the meat under the grill/broiler or on the barbecue and seal for about 8 minutes each side until it takes colour. Lower the heat and continue to grill/broil or barbecue, turning to ensure it does not burn. Cook to your taste – I think lamb should be cooked with a hint of pink in the centre.

When cooked leave to rest for 5 minutes, then slice and serve with the chermoula.

PARMESAN ICE CREAM SANDWICHES WITH CHOCOLATE BALSAMIC STRAWBERRIES

To be tasted at least once in your life…

PARMESAN ICE CREAM

500 ml/2 cups whipping cream

115 g/½ cup plus 1 tablespoon golden granulated sugar (preferably organic)

115 g/1½ cups Parmesan cheese, finely grated

CHOCOLATE BALSAMIC SAUCE

25 ml/2 tablespoons aged balsamic vinegar (Belazu is good)

2.5 g/¹⁄₁₂ oz. 100% pure cacao or 85% cacao dark/bittersweet chocolate

TO SERVE

500 g/1 lb. 2 oz. ripe, juicy strawberries, stalks removed and sliced into quarters

1 handful of basil leaves, shredded

16 of your favourite crackers or plain cookies (digestive biscuits/graham crackers are ideal)

soft whipped cream

salted caramel popcorn

SERVES 4

Bring the cream to the boil with the sugar, stirring constantly.

Remove from the heat and add the grated Parmesan cheese, stirring until it melts. Allow to cool.

Scrape the mixture into a suitable lidded container and freeze overnight.

To make the chocolate balsamic sauce, put the balsamic vinegar and cacao in a bowl and stir until well combined.

Toss the strawberries and basil in the chocolate balsamic sauce.

Remove the ice cream from the freezer. Using a hot knife cut into squares (or rectangles) slightly smaller than the size of a cracker.

Sandwich an ice cream square (or rectangle) between 2 crackers and serve with a large spoonful of chocolate strawberry mixture, a dollop of whipped cream and a sprinkling of salted caramel popcorn.

Fluffy green shells with peppery cream clouds, the former slightly warm and the latter nice and chilled, makes for a dreamy combination.

GREEN TEA MADELEINES WITH VANILLA & BLACK PEPPER CREAM

160 g/1 cup plus 2
   tablespoons plain/
   all-purpose flour
¼ teaspoon salt
½ teaspoon baking
   powder
1 tablespoon matcha
   green tea powder
   (the best quality you
   can find)
2 UK large, US extra
   large eggs
170 g/¾ cup plus
   2 tablespoons caster/
   granulated sugar
2 tablespoons freshly
   squeezed lime juice
125 g/1 stick plus
   1 tablespoon butter,
   melted and cooled
zest of 2 limes
oil, for greasing
icing/confectioners'
   sugar, for dusting

VANILLA & BLACK PEPPER CREAM
300 ml/1¼ cups
   double/heavy cream
½ vanilla pod/bean,
   seeds only
3–5 turns finely ground
   black pepper
splash of sake (optional)
icing/confectioners'
   sugar (if using sake)

2 x 9-hole madeleine pans

MAKES 18

In a medium bowl, sift together the flour, salt, baking powder and matcha powder and set aside.

In a large bowl, whisk the eggs and sugar until pale and doubled in volume, about 3–5 minutes.

Whisk the lime juice into the egg mixture then fold in the flour mixture using a spatula until just combined.

Fold in the melted butter and lime zest and refrigerate for at least 1–2 hours.

Preheat the oven to 200°C (400°F) Gas 6, when you are ready to cook the madeleines.

Grease the madeleine pans with a little oil and spoon in the batter until the mixture comes about three-quarters of the way up each mould.

Bake in the preheated oven for 12–15 minutes until the madeleines are lightly golden around the edges.

While the madeleines are cooking, make the Vanilla & Black Pepper Cream by whisking the cream into very soft peaks and folding in the vanilla and black pepper. If using the sake add a very small splash and sweeten to taste with a little icing/confectioners' sugar.

Once the madeleines are done, transfer to a wire rack to cool slightly.

Serve the warm madeleines with the cream.

I am not a natural baker and need clear and precise instructions in this category as my free-pouring savoury style does not work in the exacting, scientific realms of baking. I literally follow instructions and weights to the letter and these two books serve as my baking bibles. The cake recipe is Annie Bell's and the frosting from The Hummingbird Bakery; however, you will see that I could not resist some free-pouring and I have added a hint of Marmite (yeast extract) to the buttercream. I thought it was fabulous, but then again I am an umami nut. I suggest that when you make the buttercream, you take out a tablespoon and mix with a tiny dot of marmite before committing.

STRANGE CHOCOLATE CAKE

CAKE
225 g/2 sticks unsalted
    butter, diced
225 g/1 cup plus
    2 tablespoons golden
    caster sugar
175 g/1 cup plus
    3 tablespoons
    self-raising/self-rising
    flour, sifted
50 g/½ cup cocoa
    powder, sifted
2 teaspoons baking
    powder, sifted
¼ teaspoon fine sea salt
1 teaspoon vanilla
    extract
4 eggs
100 ml/7 tablespoons
    whole milk

CHOCOLATE MARMITE BUTTERCREAM
300 g/2½ cups
    icing/confectioners'
    sugar, sifted
100 g/1 stick minus
    1 tablespoon unsalted
    butter, at room
    temperature
40 g/3 tablespoons
    cocoa powder, sifted
40 ml/3 tablespoons
    milk
1½ teaspoons
    Marmite/yeast extract

*20-cm/8-in. non-stick
    springform cake pan,
    greased and lined with
    baking parchment*

SERVES 12

Preheat the oven to 170°C (350°F) Gas 4.

Place all the ingredients for the cake in a bowl and cream together using a handheld electric whisk or stand-alone mixer, making sure that the batter is smooth without any lumps. Pour the batter into the cake pan, smooth over the top, and bake for 40–50 minutes or until a skewer inserted into the middle of the cake comes out clean. Leave to cool.

While the cake is cooling, make the buttercream. Beat the icing/confectioners' sugar, butter, and cocoa powder together in a stand-alone mixer with a paddle attachment (or use a handheld electric whisk) on medium-slow speed until the mixture comes together and is well mixed.

With the mixer on a slower speed, add the milk to the butter mixture a couple of tablespoons at a time. Once all the milk has been incorporated, turn the mixer up to a high speed and continue beating until the buttercream is light and fluffy, about 5 minutes. The longer the buttercream is beaten, the fluffier and lighter it becomes.

Add the Marmite/yeast extract and continue beating until combined.

Once the cake has cooled, cut it in half to make two layers. On the first layer, spread one-third of the buttercream. Sandwich with the second layer of cake and spread the rest of the buttercream on top and around the sides of the cake.

When researching recipes for this section, our lovely South African intern informed us that Marmite Cake is a family favourite in that part of the world, so here it is. It's a must-try for all umami enthusiasts. I loved it, although I wondered what it would be like with a sticky toffee pudding mixture instead of the plain sponge. Nevertheless, I wanted to give you the original recipe in all its glory so you could taste it as it is supposed to be.

MARMITE (YEAST EXTRACT) CAKE

CAKE
70 g/½ stick plus
  1 tablespoon butter
170 g/¾ cup plus
  2 tablespoons sugar
1 egg, beaten
160 g/1½ cups plain/all-
  purpose flour
2 teaspoons baking powder
¼ teaspoon salt
250 ml/1 cup whole milk

TOPPING
120 g/1 stick butter
2 teaspoons Marmite/yeast
  extract
60 g/½ cup plus
  1 tablespoon grated/
  shredded Cheddar cheese

*23 x 33-cm/9 x 13-in. Pyrex
  baking dish*

SERVES 10–12

Preheat the oven to 190°C (375°F) Gas 5.

Beat the butter and sugar until light, creamy and smooth. Add the egg and beat well.

Sift the dry ingredients together. Alternate adding the dry ingredients and the milk to the butter mixture. Mix gently until well combined and the batter is smooth.

Pour the batter into the baking dish and bake in the preheated oven for 25–30 minutes.

To make the topping, simply melt the butter and mix in the Marmite/yeast extract.

Five minutes before the cake is ready, remove from the oven and prick all over with a fork. Pour over the melted butter and marmite mixture and sprinkle with the grated/shredded cheese. Return to the oven for the final 5 minutes until the cake is cooked and the cheese has melted and turned slightly golden.

This cake is best served warm from the oven.

UMAMI BLOODY MARY

This recipe was inspired by my friend Salvatore Calabrese's Bloody Asparagus recipe in his brilliant book *Cocktails By Flavour*, a must for anyone interested in the intoxicating and the enchanting.

4 fresh asparagus tips
90 ml/6 tablespoons vodka
30 ml/2 tablespoons
    Clamato juice (mix of
    tomato juice and clam
    juice) or good-quality
    tomato juice
5 ml/1 teaspoon freshly
    squeezed lemon juice
6 dashes Worcestershire
    Sauce
4 dashes Tabasco

2 pinches salt
3 twists freshly ground
    black pepper

GARNISH
saucer of soy sauce
celery salt, for dipping
2 fresh asparagus spears
1 lemon slice, cut in half

SERVES 2

Muddle the asparagus in the bottom of a cocktail shaker.

Add the remaining ingredients and ice and shake.

Dip the rim of 2 highball glasses into the soy sauce and then into the celery salt to create an umami-packed rim. Fill the glasses with ice, then strain the tomato mixture into them. Garnish with a spear of asparagus and a lemon slice.

photo of Umami Bloody Mary: page 160 (background)

PEACH & TOMATO TARTE TATIN

Umami-packed tomatoes add a cheeky twist to this classic Tarte Tatin. The tomatoes mix remarkably well with the ripe peaches.

170 g/¾ cup plus 2
    tablespoons caster/
    granulated sugar (plus
    2 tablespoons extra if
    needed)
50 g/3 tablespoons butter
400 g/14 oz. sweet cherry
    or baby plum tomatoes,
    halved
2 peaches, pitted and cut
    into 9 wedges each
1 small sprig of thyme

freshly ground black pepper
1 sheet puff pastry, rolled
    out slightly bigger than
    your pan
sour cream or a half-half
    mixture of soft goat's
    cheese and sour cream,
    to serve
*ovenproof 30-cm/12-in. Tarte
    Tatin pan*

SERVES 8–12

Preheat the oven to 200°C (400°F) Gas 6.

Put the sugar into the tarte tatin pan and place on a medium heat. Allow the sugar to melt, but shake the pan occasionally to prevent it from burning. Once melted, let it bubble until it turns a light amber-brown colour, forming a caramel. Immediately take the pan off the heat and add the butter carefully. Stir in until melted.

Arrange the tomatoes and the peaches into the pan, skin-side down into a pattern. Fit as many tomatoes as you can – you might not need them all. If your peaches are quite sharp, sprinkle over the extra 2 tablespoons of sugar. Lay the thyme over the top of the fruit and season all over with some freshly ground black pepper.

Cover with the pastry. Tuck in the edges of the pastry into the inside of the pan, including the overhang which will create a delicious crust. Prick a few small holes into the pastry with a fork. Transfer to the preheated oven and bake for 40 minutes.

Allow to cool for about 10 minutes. If there seems to be a lot of excess juice, carefully drain some off before turning the tarte out onto a serving plate. Allow the tarte to cool a little, as this allows the hot caramel to set slightly. Serve warm with sour cream or goat's cheese and sour cream mix.

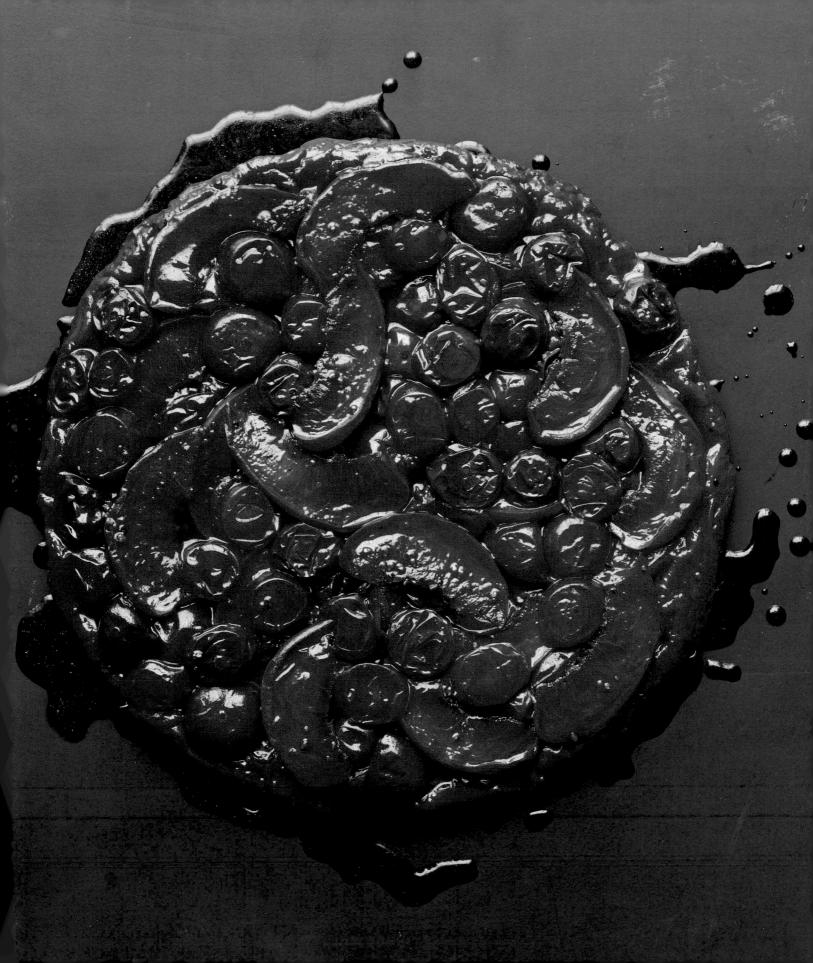

Don't make these as you will never forgive me… These biscotti are as cheesy as they are crunchy which makes them doubly addictive.

CARAWAY BISCOTTI

540 g/4 cups plain/
    all-purpose flour, plus
    extra for dusting
1 tablespoon caraway seeds
    plus 2 teaspoons to
    garnish
2 teaspoons salt
130 g/1 cup plus 1
    tablespoon Gruyère
    cheese, finely grated
130 g/1 cup Parmesan
    cheese, finely grated

2 teaspoons baking powder
¼ teaspoon cayenne pepper
¼ teaspoon mustard
    powder (optional)
170 g/1½ sticks cold,
    unsalted butter, cubed
3 UK large, US extra large
    eggs plus 1 for egg-wash
250 ml/1 cup whole milk

MAKES 60–70

Preheat the oven to 175°C (350°F) Gas 4. Make sure there are two racks available in the oven, spaced evenly.

In a large bowl, mix together the flour, 1 tablespoon caraway seeds, salt, the Gruyère and all but a small handful of Parmesan, the baking powder, cayenne pepper and mustard powder (if using). Add the butter and rub in with your fingertips until the mixture resembles breadcrumbs. Beat the 3 eggs with the milk and pour into the flour mixture. Mix together until a soft dough forms. Tip the dough out onto a floured surface and bring it together by kneading it once or twice. Quarter the dough and roll each quarter into thin, slightly flattened logs (about 5 cm/2 in. wide). Place them, spaced apart, onto baking parchment (2 logs per sheet).

Whisk the extra egg and brush over the logs. Scatter over the reserved Parmesan and remaining caraway seeds.

Bake the logs for 30 minutes in the preheated oven, switching positions and rotating the sheets 180° halfway through. The logs should be a pale golden colour and firm. Remove from the oven and allow to cool for 10 minutes. Reduce the oven temperature to 150°C (300°F) Gas 2.

Carefully slice each log into thin slices, about 1.5-cm/½-in. wide. Lay the biscotti, cut-side down, onto baking sheets and bake for 40 minutes, turning once. Cool before serving.

Kick back in the summer heat with a glass of this refreshing green tea magic. I usually take this to my deckchair with a straw and a spoon. If you want to take this healthful granita to another level, free-pour some chilled sake over the top – Kanpai!

GREEN TEA GRANITA

4 good-quality green tea
    bags, or 2 tablespoons
    loose-leaf green tea
1 handful fresh mint, finely
    chopped
2.5-cm/1-in. piece of fresh
    ginger, peeled and sliced

very small pinch of cayenne
    pepper
freshly squeezed juice of
    1 lemon
runny honey, to taste
fresh mint leaves, to serve

SERVES 4–6

Put 750 ml/3 cups water in a saucepan over a high heat. Once almost boiling, add the tea, mint, ginger and cayenne pepper then cover and turn off the heat. Leave to sit for 10 minutes to infuse then strain through a fine sieve/strainer to remove the solids.

Add the lemon juice and honey to taste.

Pour the liquid into a plastic or glass container and place in the freezer for at least 3–4 hours. It is important that every 30 minutes you stir the mixture with a fork to break up the ice crystals.

When ready to serve, if you find the mixture is too slushy, give it a good stir and return to the freezer until more solid, or if you find it is too hard just remove it from the freezer for a few minutes until softened slightly.

Serve in glasses garnished with fresh mint leaves.

This recipe is my take on Anna Hansen's fabulous Pumpkin and Miso Cheesecake. In order to add to the umami in the miso, I swapped out the pumpkin for sweet potatoes (sweet potatoes have more umami than pumpkin), reduced the sugar and added the lime to give it some citrus freshness. Don't be sad if this cheesecake cracks – this is the case for most baked cheesecakes, so it's best to accept and expect imperfect perfection.

MISO & SWEET POTATO CHEESECAKE

300 ml/2¼ cups double/heavy cream, whipped, to serve

ROASTED SWEET POTATO PURÉE
750 g/1⅔ lbs. raw sweet potato, skin on and cut into chunks
olive oil

BASE
120 g/4¼ oz. digestive biscuits/graham crackers
140 g/5 oz. ginger biscuits/cookies
1 tablespoon muscovado sugar
120 g/1 stick butter, plus extra for greasing

FILLING
500 g/2 cups plus 3 tablespoons cream cheese
60 g/4 tablespoons white miso paste
150 g/¾ cup caster/granulated sugar
1 vanilla pod/bean, seeds only
freshly squeezed juice of 1 lime
zest of 2 limes
1 quantity Roasted Sweet Potato Purée (see left)
5 eggs
2 extra egg yolks

23-cm/9-in. springform cake pan, lined with baking parchment and greased thoroughly

SERVES 8–12

Preheat the oven to 200°C (400°F) Gas 6.

Start with the Roasted Sweet Potato Purée: toss the sweet potatoes with a drizzle of oil on a baking sheet and roast in the preheated oven for about 40 minutes.

Allow it to cool for a little while and peel of the skin. Place in a food processor and blitz until smooth.

Next, make the base: blitz the digestive biscuits/graham crackers and ginger biscuits/cookies and the sugar to a medium-fine crumb in a food processor. Melt the butter and add to the biscuit/cookie crumbs. Pulse until just mixed. Tip the mixture into the cake pan, then press it evenly into the bottom of the pan. Bake for 10 minutes then leave to cool.

Turn the oven down to 180°C (350°F) Gas 4. Clean the bowl of the food processor. Add the cream cheese, miso paste, sugar, vanilla seeds, lime juice and zest and blend until smooth, scraping down the sides of the bowl. Add the Roasted Sweet Potato Purée, eggs and extra yolks and blend again until smooth, making sure you scrape down the sides of the bowl once more.

Pour this mixture into the cake pan and bake for 15 minutes. Reduce the temperature to 110°C (225°F) Gas ¼ and bake for a further 60–70 minutes. The cake is ready when it is set around the edges and slightly wobbly in the centre.

Remove from the oven and leave the cheesecake to cool in its pan on a wire rack for about 1 hour. Then, run a knife around the edges of the pan and carefully remove the ring. Slide the cheesecake onto a plate and leave to cool completely before serving.

Serve with whipped double/heavy cream.

FIG & WALNUT BISCOTTI

I have adapted this delicious treat from one of my favourite Smitten Kitchen recipes...

85 g/6 tablespoons unsalted butter, softened

50 g/¼ cup granulated sugar, plus extra for sprinkling

75 g/5 tablespoons dark brown sugar

2 eggs

1 teaspoon vanilla extract

finely grated zest of ½ large orange

255 g/scant 2 cups plain/all-purpose flour

¼ teaspoon salt

1 teaspoon baking powder

¼ teaspoon bicarbonate of/baking soda

1 teaspoon ground cinnamon

1 teaspoon ground ginger

¼ teaspoon ground nutmeg

⅛ teaspoon ground cloves

60 g/½ cup walnut halves, roughly chopped and toasted

180 g/1 cup plus 2 tablespoons dried figs, roughly chopped

3 tablespoons finely chopped rosemary

1 egg white, lightly beaten

MAKES APPROX. 24

Preheat the oven to 165°C (325°F) Gas 3.

In the bowl of an electric mixer, cream the butter and sugars together until fluffy. Add the eggs, one at a time, scraping down the sides of the bowl after every addition. Beat until well mixed then beat in the vanilla and orange zest.

In another bowl, sift together the flour, salt, baking powder, bicarbonate of/baking soda, cinnamon, ginger, nutmeg and cloves. Tip them into the butter mixture and beat until a firm-ish dough is formed. Add the walnuts, figs and rosemary and beat until well combined. Tip the dough onto clingfilm/plastic wrap, and chill until completely firm (35–40 minutes).

Once firm, lightly grease a baking sheet. Divide the dough into two and roll each piece into a log, about 30 cm/12 in. long and 10 cm/4 in. wide. Place them on the baking sheet. Brush with the beaten egg white and sprinkle with sugar.

Bake in the preheated oven for 15–20 minutes or until the logs are golden brown. Remove and allow to cool for 10 minutes. With a serrated knife, cut each log into slices, about 1–1.5-cm/½-in. thick and lay them, sliced-side down, onto the baking sheet and return to the oven for a further 20 minutes until toasted and crisp. Let them cool before serving.

Rich and dark, this unusual pairing capitalizes on the fact that wine experts have detected umami in rich, full-bodied red wines. The addition of the chocolate turns a holiday favourite into a year-round treat. Make sure you use a good, drinkable wine, as it will make a difference. Pairing it with the Fig & Walnut Biscotti adds another lovely angle, and if you really want to drive your guests wild, include a glistening plate of frozen grapes (yes you literally just wash them and pop them in the freezer!).

RICH CHOCOLATE MULLED WINE

1 x 70-cl/24-fl. oz. bottle full-bodied bottle red wine

1 cinnamon stick

1 teaspoon ground allspice

5 whole cloves

140 g/5 oz. 100% pure cacao or 85% cacao dark/bittersweet chocolate

3 tablespoons soft brown sugar or honey or to taste

SERVES 6–8

Warm the red wine and bring it to a simmer (do not boil). Add the spices, then the cacao and finally the sugar or honey.

Pour the wine into heat-resistant glasses and serve immediately with Fig & Walnut Biscotti.

STOCKS & BROTHS

SIMPLE CHICKEN SOUP

1 whole large chicken, preferably organic with giblets

2 Spanish onions, quartered

2 celery stalks, each snapped in two

2 small or 1 large carrot(s), cut in two

2 leeks, cut in two and well rinsed

2 sprigs flat-leaf parsley

2 sprigs fresh thyme

1 large bay leaf

3 garlic cloves

½ teaspoon black peppercorns

1 tablespoon rock salt

orzo pasta or rice

2 handfuls of shredded kale or white cabbage

Parmesan cheese, to serve

SERVES 8

Put the chicken in a tall pan with the other ingredients. Fill with cold water until the chicken is completely covered, about 3 litres/quarts. Bring to the boil, lower the heat and simmer gently for about 1 hour 20 minutes, or until the liquid is a flavoursome broth and the chicken is falling apart. Adjust the seasoning and drain the liquid into a separate pan. Remove the chicken and giblets and set aside to cool. Discard the vegetables and herbs.

Pick the meat from the cooled chicken and set aside. To feed 4–5, drain off half the soup. This can be stored in the fridge or freezer when cool. I keep mine in the fridge and use it for supper later in the week. Bring the rest to the boil and add 1–2 handfuls of pasta or rice per person and one for the pot. Follow pasta cooking times and about 1 minute before the pasta is due to be ready add the kale or cabbage and a handful of chicken meat per person.

I chop the giblets and add them to my bowl, but other family members aren't so keen. Therefore check out your audience, before adding these contentious nuggets to the general pot. Serve in large bowls with grated Parmesan cheese.

BASIC STOCK

raw or cooked chicken carcass or 1–2 kg/2¼–4½ lbs. raw or cooked bones from a roast OR 1–2 kg/ 2¼–4½ lbs. beef bones or a mixture of the two (raw giblets can also be added)

½ head garlic, unpeeled and bashed

1 large onion, unpeeled and quartered

2 celery sticks, roughly chopped

1 leek, roughly chopped

1 large carrot, peeled and roughly chopped

2 bay leaves

any fresh herbs, such as thyme, parsley etc.

5 whole black peppercorns

1 tablespoon coarse sea salt

MAKES 600–1,200 ML/ 1–2 PINTS

Put all the ingredients in a large, heavy-based pan and cover with water. Bring to the boil and then turn down to a simmer. Continue to cook gently for about 3–4 hours, continuously skimming off any scum that comes to the surface. Pass through a fine sieve/strainer and leave to cool. You can store this in the fridge for about 3 days and it also freezes really well for up to 3 months. Store it in smaller containers so you only have to defrost what you need.

MISO POTASSIUM BROTH

7 medium organic potatoes (peelings only cut to ½-cm/¼-in deep)

3 parsnips (peelings only cut to ½-cm/¼-in deep)

6 celery stalks

1 bunch of flat-leaf parsley

10-cm/4-in. piece ginger

3 litres/12 cups of water

brown organic miso paste

MAKES APPROX. 2 LITRES/8 CUPS

Put all the ingredients in a large heavy-based saucepan and cover with lots of water. Aim for about approximately one part vegetables to four parts water. Bring to the boil then with the lid on and simmer for 1–2 hours. Season to taste with brown organic miso paste. Strain and allow to cool before refrigerating.

UMAMI BONE BROTH

8 kg/18 lbs. beef bones
(a mix of bone marrow,
oxtail, short ribs, neck
bones or shanks)
2 tablespoons olive oil
2 tablespoons tomato
purée/paste
2 onions, peeled and
roughly chopped
2 leeks, roughly chopped
2 carrots, peeled and
roughly chopped

1 head garlic, cut in half
horizontally
1 handful dried shiitake
mushrooms
2 bay leaves
1 bunch flat-leaf parsley
6 sprigs thyme
1 tablespoon whole black
peppercorns
1 tablespoon cider vinegar

**MAKES APPROX.
3 LITRES/12 CUPS**

Preheat the oven to 200°C (400°F) Gas 6. Place the beef
bones in a roasting tray and drizzle with olive oil and rub all
over with tomato purée/paste. Roast until well browned, for
approximately 30 minutes.

Transfer the bones (and any juices) into a large, heavy-based
saucepan and add all the other ingredients and enough cold
water to cover by about 5 cm/2 in.

Cover the pan and bring to the boil. Reduce the heat to a
very low simmer and cook with lid slightly ajar, occasionally
skimming off any scum, for at least 8 but up to 24 hours.
The longer you simmer it, the better your stock will be.
Make sure the bones and vegetables are completely
submerged – top up with more water if you need to.

Once done, remove the pan from the heat and let cool for
about 30 minutes. Strain the broth through a fine-mesh
sieve/strainer or muslin/cheesecloth and discard the bones
and vegetables. Leave until completely cooled then divide
into smaller containers and refrigerate. Before using, remove
any solidified fat from the top of the chilled broth.

Alternatively, you can cook the broth in a slow cooker
on low for the same amount of time.

Season before serving. You can use simple Braggs Liquid
Aminos, Himalayan pink salt, Marmite, miso, Umami
Bomb/Paste…

DIPS & DRESSINGS

UMAMI VINAIGRETTE

2 tablespoons soy sauce
2 tablespoons toasted
sesame oil
2 teaspoons rice vinegar
juice of 2 limes
2.5-cm/1-in. piece fresh
ginger, finely grated

2–3 teaspoons runny honey
(or to taste)
good pinch cayenne pepper
(or to taste)

SERVES 8

Simply whisk all the ingredients together.

TASTY TOMATO SALSA

approx. 16–17 whole cherry
tomatoes
1 garlic clove
1 heaped tablespoon capers
1 heaped tablespoon
stoned/pitted black olives
2 anchovy fillets in olive oil,
drained
½ red onion, finely chopped

1 handful chopped mint,
basil or flat-leaf parsley
or a bit of all three
3 tablespoons extra virgin
olive oil
juice of ½ lemon
salt flakes and freshly
ground black pepper

SERVES 8

Pulse all ingredients in a food processor until they form an
easily spooned dip, but do not over-process and try to retain
some of the texture of the ingredients. Season to taste.

CLASSIC CAESAR DRESSING

2–3 garlic cloves
1 tablespoon Dijon mustard
1 tablespoon white wine
  vinegar
salt and freshly ground
  black pepper
2 heaped tablespoons
  mayonnaise
1 tablespoon Taste #5
  Umami Bomb/Paste
  Original Recipe

4 tablespoons extra virgin
  olive oil
1 tablespoon finely grated,
  Parmesan cheese
dash of Worcestershire
  sauce
squeeze lemon juice

SERVES 4

Blend the garlic, mustard and vinegar with a couple of pinches of salt in a food processor. Add the mayonnaise and Umami Bomb/Paste and blend. Slowly add the oil in a steady stream until the mixture has a thick dressing consistency.

Fold in the Parmesan cheese using a spatula and season with salt, pepper, Worcestershire sauce and a squeeze of lemon.

UMAMI HUMMUS

2 x 400-g/14-oz cans
  chickpeas
1–2 garlic cloves, crushed
6 tablespoons tahini paste
1 tablespoon sundried
  tomato paste or Taste #5
  Umami Bomb/Paste
  Original Recipe
handful green olives,
  drained and stoned/pitted
juice of 1 lemon

4 ice cubes
6 tablespoons extra virgin
  olive oil (plus some extra
  to serve)
sea salt and freshly ground
  black pepper
flat-leaf parsley, finely
  chopped, to garnish

SERVES 6–8

Rinse the chickpeas in cold water and put into a food processor with all the other ingredients apart from the oil.

Turn on the food processor, add the ice cubes and slowly trickle in the oil. Blitz until smooth, creamy and pale in colour. Season with salt and black pepper.

To serve drizzle with more olive oil and sprinkle with parsley.

TONNATO DIP OR DRESSING

250 ml/1 cup mayonnaise
100 g/⅔ cup canned tuna in
  olive oil, drained
yolks of 2 hard-boiled eggs
2 anchovy fillets in olive oil,
  drained or a squeeze of
  Taste #5 Umami
  Bomb/Paste Original
  Recipe

1 tablespoon capers
  in vinegar, drained
3 pickled cucumbers/
  gherkins
squeeze lemon juice
sea salt and ground white
  pepper

SERVES 6

Put all the ingredients except the lemon juice, salt and pepper in a food processor and whizz to combine. Let the mixture down with the lemon juice until is thinner but not runny. Season to taste.

CANNELINI BEAN
& PROSCIUTTO DIP

400-g/14-oz. can cannellini
  beans, drained and rinsed
65 g/4 slices lean prosciutto
  di Parma (fat removed)
45 g/¾ cup Parmesan
  cheese, finely grated
salt flakes and freshly
  ground black pepper
a handful flat-leaf parsley

180 ml/¾ cup extra virgin
  olive oil
zest and juice of ½ lemon
  juice
sea salt and freshly ground
  black pepper

SERVES 4

In a food processor blend all the ingredients together apart from the olive oil. Slowly drizzle in the olive oil to combine, and add a little water if the mixture is too stiff when blending. Serve drizzled with a little more olive oil and a squeeze of lemon.

SIMPLE SAUCES & GRAVY

REALLY RED SAUCE

1 onion, quartered
2 carrots, quartered
2 celery stalks, quartered
3 garlic cloves
2 tablespoons olive oil
3 x 400-g/14-oz. cans
    chopped tomatoes

3 tablespoons Taste #5
    Umami Bomba! **XXX**
    (optional)
large handful basil leaves
sea salt and freshly ground
    black pepper
1 teaspoon sugar

SERVES 8

Pulse the onion, carrots, celery and garlic in a food processor until everything is chopped to the size of small red lentils.

Heat the oil in a large pan/skillet, add the vegetables, and sauté in the oil until the onion becomes translucent – do not allow the mixture to colour.

Add the tomatoes (I always fill a third of the can with water to wash out any lingering pieces and add some extra liquid), Umami Bomba! XXX, torn basil leaves, salt, pepper and sugar.

Cook over a low heat, stirring frequently, for 20–30 minutes.

BBQ SAUCE

6 tablespoons balsamic
    vinegar
6 tablespoons soy sauce
6 tablespoons honey
6 tablespoons tomato
    ketchup
1 tablespoon Taste #5
    Umami Bomb/Paste
    Original Recipe

3 garlic cloves, peeled
    and bruised
2 fresh red chillies/chiles,
    split open and deseeded

**COATS APPROX. 8
CHICKEN DRUMSTICKS**

Combine all the ingredients in a bowl to use as a marinade for chicken, steaks, ribs…

Alternatively, simmer in a pan for 10–15 minutes and use to smother over cooked meats or use as a dipping sauce.

WHITE SAUCE/CHEESE SAUCE

575 ml/2⅓ cups whole milk
50 g/3 tablespoons plain/
    all-purpose flour
60 g/½ stick butter
nutmeg, grated (optional)
2 teaspoons Taste #5
    Umami Bomb/Paste
    Original Recipe
sea salt and freshly ground
    black pepper

CHEESE SAUCE

70 g/1 scant cup Cheddar
    cheese, grated/shredded
40 g/½ cup Parmesan
    cheese, grated

SERVES 4

Place the milk, flour and butter in a medium saucepan. Gradually bring to simmering point, whisking continuously, for about 5 minutes, or until the sauce becomes thick and smooth.

Reduce the heat to low, and allow the sauce to cook very gently for 5 minutes, stirring occasionally.

Season the sauce with a small grating of nutmeg (if using), salt and freshly ground black pepper.

To make a cheese sauce, simply add the cheeses at the end. Stir until melted.

MARIE ROSE SAUCE

250 ml/1 cup mayonnaise
3 tablespoons tomato
    ketchup
1 tablespoon
    Worcestershire sauce
1 tablespoon Cognac

1 tablespoon Sherry
dash of Tabasco sauce
squeeze of lemon juice
pinch of paprika

SERVES 6–8

Mix all the ingredients together. This sauce needs to be a delicate pale pink, so adjust the colour by adding more mayonnaise or ketchup accordingly.

UMAMI PESTO

2 large handfuls of your
  favourite herbs
  (leaves only)
1–2 garlic cloves
1–2 tablespoons walnuts,
  toasted in a dry
  pan/skillet and roughly
  chopped
2 anchovies in oil, drained
3 sundried tomatoes in oil,
  drained and finely
  chopped

1 tablespoon black olives,
  stoned/pitted
grated zest and squeeze
  of juice from 1 lemon
sea salt and freshly ground
  black pepper
30 g/scant ½ cup Pecorino
  cheese, grated
30 g/scant ½ cup Parmesan
  cheese, grated
good extra virgin olive oil

SERVES 4–6

Place the herbs, garlic, walnuts, anchovies, sundried tomatoes, olives and lemon zest in a mortar with a small pinch of sea salt. Crush the ingredients together to release their flavours, taking care not to be rough as this will spoil the texture of the finished pesto.

Add the cheeses. Pour in a steady stream of oil, stirring until you reach your chosen consistency. Season to taste with a squeeze of lemon and more salt and pepper. Instead of using a pestle and mortar, you can pulse all the ingredients in a food processor, but take care not to spoil the texture.

UMAMI MAYONNAISE

4 tablespoons mayonnaise
2 teaspoons Taste #5
  Umami Bomb/Paste
  Vegetarian Recipe
2 tablespoons spring
  onions/scallions, finely
  chopped

1 tablespoon
  coriander/cilantro,
  finely chopped
squeeze of lime juice
sea salt and freshly ground
  black pepper

SERVES 4

Simply mix all the ingredients together.

QUICK CAPER & ANCHOVY SAUCE

13 anchovy fillets packed in
  olive oil (i.e. 1 small jar or
  can), drained and finely
  chopped
⅔ cup extra virgin olive oil,
  divided in half
3 tablespoons capers, finely
  chopped
juice from 1 lemon and
  a grating of lemon zest

1 handful flat-leaf parsley,
  finely chopped
½ teaspoon chilli/hot red
  pepper flakes
salt and freshly ground
  black pepper, if necessary

SERVES 6–8

Add the anchovies and half the olive oil into a small pan and heat on a very low heat until the anchovies have melted into the oil. Remove from the heat and add the rest of the ingredients and serve. If you don't mind your anchovies chunky (I love them), you can leave out the melting stage and just mix all the ingredients together.

This sauce can be stored in the fridge for up to a week. It will solidify in the fridge so be sure to take it out before you wish to use it, to allow time for the oil to reach room temperature.

MIRACLE GRAVY

2 tablespoons vegetable oil
30 g/2 tablespoons plain/
  all-purpose flour
570 ml/2⅓ cups good-
  quality chicken stock
140 ml/5 fl. oz. port
  (or wine or Sherry)

2 tablespoons redcurrant jelly
2 tablespoons Taste #5
  Umami Bomb/Paste
  Original Recipe
salt and freshly ground
  black pepper

SERVES 8

In a large saucepan, heat the oil over a medium heat and stir in the flour. Cook for 1 minute.

Gradually pour in the stock and port, whisking all the time.

Add the redcurrant jelly and Umami Bomb/Paste, mixing through well.

Bring to the boil then reduce to simmer for 2–3 minutes. Season to taste.

SALTS, SPRINKLES & RUBS

UMAMI SALT

ground porcini mushrooms
ground sea salt flakes
ground black pepper

freeze-dried flat-leaf parsley
and/or basil

Combine roughly the same quantity of porcini and sea salt flakes and season with some black pepper and parsley and/or basil.

GREEN TEA & SHIITAKE MUSHROOM SALT

1–2 tablespoons salt flakes
3 large dried shiitake
mushrooms
1 nori sheet, broken into
small pieces

1 heaped teaspoon
Genmaicha green tea

SERVES 8–10

Blend the ingredients in a coffee grinder. Store in an airtight container.

BURNT WALNUT & BLUE CHEESE BUTTER

100 g/7 tablespoons
softened salted butter
1 tablespoon chopped flat
leaf-parsley
150 g/1¼ cups strong blue
cheese (Roquefort,
Gorgonzola Piccante etc)

75 g/¾ cup toasted walnuts,
finely chopped
a dash of port (optional)
sea salt and freshly ground
black pepper

SERVES 15–20

In a bowl, cream the butter with the other ingredients. Adjust the seasoning and roll the mixture into a sausage shape. Wrap in clingfilm/plastic wrap and chill in the fridge until firm. Cut into coin-shaped slices and use to top grilled meats and fish.

BASIC UMAMI RUB

1 onion, peeled and
quartered
1 bunch rosemary, leaves
only
1 bunch sage, leaves only
1 handful flat-leaf parsley
2 garlic cloves, peeled
olive oil
sea salt and freshly ground
black pepper

Aromat (if you are MSG-
sensitive, replace with
Taste #5 Umami
Bomb/Paste Original
Recipe, soy sauce, or
1–2 anchovies in oil)

**MAKES ENOUGH FOR
1 WHOLE CHICKEN
OR 4–6 STEAKS**

Place all the ingredients, except the Aromat, salt and pepper in a food processor with a little olive oil and pulse until chopped into little pieces – not a pulp. Add more oil to make a runny paste.

Season to taste with salt, pepper and Aromat.

Use this rub as a marinade or rub before roasting or BBQ-ing.

PANGRATATTO SPRINKLE

60 ml/¼ cup olive oil
100 g/2 cups sourdough
breadcrumbs
zest of 1 lemon
2 garlic cloves, crushed
1 tablespoon finely grated
aged Pecorino cheese

3 tablespoons flat-leaf
parsley, finely chopped
1 tablespoon ground Taste
#5 Umami Pepper, or a
mix of nutritional yeast
and ground black pepper

SERVES 4–6

Put a frying pan/skillet over a medium heat and add the oil. Once warmed, add the breadcrumbs, lemon zest, garlic and toss together. Fry until crunchy and deep golden. Cool slightly and then add the herbs, cheese and pepper.

Enjoy sprinkled on vegetables, pasta dishes or stews.

SNACKS

UMAMI SWIRLS

1 pack ready-rolled puff
pastry
100 g/1¼ cups extra strong
hard cheese, such as
Cheddar, Parmesan,
Pecorino, grated

1 generous dessert spoon
yeast extract, such as
Marmite or Vegemite, or
1 generous tablespoon
Taste #5 Umami Bomb/
Paste Original Recipe

MAKES 15

Preheat the oven to 190°C (375°F) Gas 4.

Remove the pastry from the fridge 15–20 minutes before
use. Line 2 baking sheets with greaseproof paper.

Unroll the pastry and spread the yeast extract over the
pastry, spreading right to the edges. Sprinkle over the cheese
and roll into a long cylinder from the longer edge. Cut the
cylinder into even-sized pieces (about 15) and lay flat on the
baking sheets. Leave enough space around each wheel as the
pastry will expand and you don't want them sticking together.

Bake for 15 minutes or until golden brown and slightly crispy.
Leave to cool on the trays for a couple of minutes and then
transfer to a wire rack with a fish slice.

UMAMI POPCORN

4 tablespoons sunflower or
vegetable oil
100 g/½ cup popping corn
kernels

100 g/7 tablespoons butter,
melted
Taste #5 Umami Rush

SERVES 2

Put the oil and corn in a heavy-based pot with a tight-fitting
lid over a medium heat. Put the lid on and heat, shaking
occasionally, until the corn kernels start to pop. Turn up the
heat and shake frequently. Try not to lift off the lid too early
otherwise the popcorn will escape! Once the popping slows
down to about 2–3 seconds between pops, remove from the
heat and pour into a large bowl. Remove any unpopped or
partially popped kernels you see. Pour over the melted
butter and sprinkle generously with Umami Rush to serve.

PEPPERED MUSHROOM CRISPS

300 g/10½ oz. 'meaty
mushrooms', such as
Portobello or king oyster
olive oil

salt and Taste #5 Umami
Pepper or freshly ground
black pepper

SERVES 2–4

Preheat the oven to 150°C (300°F) Gas 2.

Use a mandoline or sharp knife to slice mushrooms into
thin slices about 4 cm/1½ in. thick.

If you are not a using non-stick baking sheet, line a couple
of baking sheets with parchment. Make sure that the
mushroom slices are really dry and place on the sheets,
leaving a little space between mushrooms.

Brush each mushroom with a little olive oil on both sides and
season with umami pepper if using or simply salt and pepper.
Bake in the preheated oven one tray at a time until slices are
dark but not burnt and crispy.

INDEX

SENIOR DESIGNER Megan Smith
COMMISSIONING EDITOR Nathan Joyce
INFOGRAPHIC DESIGNER Maria Lee-Warren
HEAD OF PRODUCTION Patricia Harrington
ART DIRECTOR Leslie Harrington
EDITORIAL DIRECTOR Julia Charles
PUBLISHER Cindy Richards

FOOD & PROP STYLIST Simon Andrews
INDEXER Vanessa Bird

First published in 2015 by Ryland Peters & Small 20–21 Jockey's Fields, London WC1R 4BW and 341 E 116th St New York NY 10029

www.rylandpeters.com

Text © Laura Santtini 2015
Design and photographs © Ryland Peters & Small 2015

ISBN: 978-1-84975-667-9

Printed and bound in China

10 9 8 7 6 5 4 3 2 1

A CIP record for this book is available from the British Library.

US Library of Congress Cataloging-in-Publication Data has been applied for.

AUTHOR'S NOTES
• At the time of going to print all the fish and seafood included in this book was available in a sustainable format. Please liaise with your fishmonger or check out www.fishonline.org for further information.

• On page 8, I have included two products containing Monosodium Glutamate (MSG) as a mark of respect to the important and valuable work of Professor Kikunae Ikeda, without whose discovery of the existence of umami in 1908 this book would never have been written.

Professor Ikeda then went on to develop MSG, which today has become a controversial subject. Despite this, the two products I have listed that contain MSG remain popular with home cooks around the world. I believe that as a flavourist and not a scientist my job is to provide a complete guide covering all available sources of umami for home cooks. I also believe in a free world and free information allowing informed decisions to be made. I have also included plenty of umami packed ingredients including my own range that are packed with naturally occurring umami and do not contain MSG. None of the recipes in this book require MSG or ingredients containing MSG. Build the umami larder that suits your beliefs, your body and your taste buds.

THE TASTE #5 UMAMI STORY

My only claim to fame in this world is inventing the world's first umami paste. Having studied, if not scrutinized umami to the point of obsession, searching for the instant benefits it can bring to a home cook's repertoire, it seemed crazy to me that a simple scratch-cooking ingredient with all this valuable magic rolled into one squeeze did not exist. So strong was my belief that I literally put our money where my mouth was at and sold our home to fund the manufacture of the first magic tube in 2009.

The journey has not been without white knuckles and many many, complications, disappointments and of course great joys and excitement. Even withstanding two earthquakes and a tsunami, we have still in our small way managed to peddle over 1 million tubes of deliciousness across the globe. My quest to create useful pantry tools for everyday transformation continues and my Taste #5 Umami range has now grown to a small family of five and expanding.

I am so grateful to all those home cooks who have supported my journey past, present and future. Thank you from the heart.

For more information on the Taste #5 Umami Collection and quick and easy basic recipes from quick dips to basic sauces and marinades, you can find more recipes on my website: WWW.LAURASANTTINI.COM

TASTE #5 UMAMI FLAVOUR BOMB COLLECTION:
Taste #5 Umami Bomb/Paste, Original Tomato
Taste #5 Umami Bomb/Paste, Vegetarian Garlic
Taste #5 Umami Bomba! XXX Tomato Purée/Paste
Taste #5 Umami Rush
Taste #5 Umami Pepper

Understanding umami makes non-cooks good,
good cooks great and great cooks extraordinary.

ACKNOWLEDGMENTS

Many thanks to: my best friend and love Skolls and our family Mathilda, Giacomo, Josie and Pudding for general deliciousness and making home my favourite place to be. My father Gino Santin for making umami an instinctive part of my cooking. Con Poulos for his magical photography and delivering something visually way more beautiful than the sum of its parts. Chloe for all her help and support and for always being one step ahead. Anel for being so helpful and sweet in such a savoury context. Kim Yorio, my partner and friend, and all at YC Media NYC. Roux for special effects and generally making things pop. Simon Andrews for the 'drool factor' – his brilliant food styling takes deliciousness to a whole new level. Dr Kumiko Ninomiya for her support and wealth of scientific knowledge. To Greg and Susan Stamm for caring and believing. The incredible team at Ryland Peters & Small: Cindy Richards, Nathan Joyce, Leslie Harrington and Megan Smith for a super positive and highly enjoyable publishing experience.